CREDO: I BELIEVE

CREDO: I BELIEVE

Faith and Life Series

BOOK FIVE

Ignatius Press, San Francisco
Catholics United for the Faith, New Rochelle

Nihil Obstat: James T. O'Connor, S.T.D.
                Censor Librorum
Imprimatur: + Joseph T. O'Keefe, D.D.
                Vicar General, New York

Director: Rev. Msgr. Eugene Kevane, Ph.D.
Assistant Director and General Editor: Patricia I. Puccetti, M.A.
Writer: Daria M. Sockey

Catholics United for the Faith, Inc., and Ignatius Press gratefully acknowledge the guidance and assistance of Reverend Monsignor Eugene Kevane, former Director of the Pontifical Catechetical Institute, Diocese of Arlington, Virginia, in the production of this series. The series intends to implement the authentic approach in Catholic catechesis given to the Church in the recent documents of the Holy See and in particular the Conference of Joseph Cardinal Ratzinger on "Sources and Transmission of Faith".

CONTENTS

APPENDIX

PART ONE

God,
The Father of All

CHAPTER 1

I Believe

What is faith? Many of the stories we enjoyed when we were younger talk about the importance of ''faith'', or ''believing''. ''If more children would believe in fairies, then Tinkerbell would come back to life'', says Peter Pan. Remember *The Little Engine That Could*? The little engine was able to pull an enormous train when the bigger engines failed. He repeated over and over to himself, ''I think I can.'' By believing that he could pull the train over the mountain, the little engine made his wish come true.

But that is not the kind of faith we are talking about here. Fairy tale heroes make things come true by having ''faith'' in them. But truths about God, about ourselves, and about God's Church are real and true whether we believe them or not. For us, faith is a gift that God gives us. This gift is the power to believe what God tells us about himself and about the world he made. We receive the gift of faith at Baptism. Because most of us have had the gift of faith since we were babies, we often take it for granted. We find it easy to believe what we are taught in religion class. We don't realize that it is only because of God's help that we can believe so easily. But if you think about it, because they are mysteries, many of the truths we believe cannot be accepted by the human mind alone. We cannot possibly understand completely how God can be three Persons but only one God. We cannot ''prove'' by scientific experiment that Jesus Christ is both God and man. We need faith in order to believe these things. And since God has shown us his wisdom and love so many times in human history, we know we can trust him to tell us the truth, even if at times it is hard to understand.

Now that you are older, you will begin to notice that much of the world around you is without faith. Many people have never been baptized and have not received the gift of faith. Many others have chosen to turn away from the faith they once had. You must ask God each day to keep your own faith strong; as you grow older you will probably find many people, books, and TV shows that will try to convince you that the life of faith is not mature and grown up. If you ask him, God will help you to keep following him instead of an unbelieving crowd.

The Apostles' Creed

We also use the word *faith* in another way. Besides being the power to believe, it also means *what* we believe. When we speak of ''the Catholic faith'', we mean ''all that we Catholics believe''.

If someone who is not a Catholic asked you, ''Can you tell me everything you believe?'', you might not know where to start. But the Church has given us a quick, orderly way of saying what it is we believe. This is the *Apostles' Creed*. The Apostles' Creed contains the most important truths of our faith. It starts right at the beginning with our belief that there is a God, and that he is the almighty Creator of Heaven and earth. It goes on to tell what we believe about God's Son, who came to earth to save us from our sins. The last part of the Creed expresses our belief that God the Holy Spirit continues to work in the world through the Catholic Church. When we say the Creed we are making a "profession" of our faith. That is, we are standing up for what we believe.

In this book we will be examining the Creed to see what we can discover about our faith. You have learned quite a lot of the faith in earlier grades. But in this book we will take a deeper, more careful look at what we believe, so that when you say the Creed you can do so more intelligently, understanding what you are saying and meaning what you are saying.

THE APOSTLES' CREED

I believe in God, the Father almighty, Creator of Heaven and earth; and in Jesus Christ, his only Son, Our Lord, who was conceived by the Holy Spirit, born of the Virgin Mary, suffered under Pontius Pilate, was crucified, died, and was buried. He descended into Hell; the third day he rose again from the dead. He ascended into Heaven, and is seated at the right hand of God, the Father almighty. From thence he shall come to judge the living and the dead.

I believe in the Holy Spirit, the Holy Catholic Church, the Communion of Saints, the forgiveness of sins, the resurrection of the body, and life everlasting. *Amen.*

Words to Know:

faith   Apostles' Creed
mystery   revelation

> Faith is the beginning of the Christian Man.
>
> — St. Ambrose

Q. 1   *What are the truths revealed by God?*

The truths revealed by God are chiefly those summarized in the Apostles' Creed. They are called truths of faith because we must believe them, with full faith, as taught by God, who can neither deceive nor be deceived.

Q. 2   *What is the Apostles' Creed?*

The Apostles' Creed is a profession of faith in the chief mysteries and the other truths revealed by God through Jesus Christ and his apostles, and taught by the Church.

Q. 3   *What is a mystery?*

A mystery is a truth entirely above our reason, but not contrary to it, which we believe because God has revealed it.

Q. 4   *What are the chief mysteries of faith that we profess in the Creed?*

The chief mysteries professed in the Creed are two: the Unity and Trinity of God; and the Incarnation, Passion, and death of Our Lord Jesus Christ.

Q. 5   *Are these two chief mysteries of faith professed and expressed also in another way?*

Yes, we profess and express these two chief mysteries of the faith also with the Sign of the Cross, which therefore is the sign of a Christian.

Q. 6 *How is the Sign of the Cross made?*

The Sign of the Cross is made by placing the right hand at the forehead, saying: ''In the name of the Father''; then the hand is placed at the breast, saying: ''and of the Son''; then the hand touches the left and the right shoulders, saying: ''and of the Holy Spirit''; and it ends with the word ''*Amen*''.

Q. 7 *How do we express the two chief mysteries of the faith by the Sign of the Cross?*

By the Sign of the Cross, we express the Unity and Trinity of God with the words; and by tracing the cross with our hand, we express the Passion and death of Our Lord Jesus Christ.

CHAPTER 2

The Trinity

The very first truth we hold by faith is that God exists. Now this truth can also be known without faith; man can reach it by his reason. What matters is not how we come to know or believe it but what it means to us, how we respond to it. You see, so many people treat this truth with indifference. But once you seriously admit that God exists it turns everything around. What matters is no longer just *me* but *God*. His will matters, not just mine; his plans, not just mine.

Many times people ask, ''Wasn't it boring for God before he made Heaven and earth? He was all by himself, with nothing to do or see and no place to go.''

If you have ever had this thought, it is because you are thinking that God is just like you. Yes, if *you* had to be by yourself from all eternity, you would be bored to death. That is because you are not perfect. As a perfect being, God needs only himself to be happy.

What does it mean to be a perfect being? Since all we really know are our own imperfect selves, it is hard to understand what ''perfection'' is. But if we think about our *im*perfections and then remember that God does not have them, we will begin to understand.

No matter how hard we try, we all commit sins some time or another. But God is *all-holy*; he cannot do or think any evil.

There are many things we cannot do because we are not strong or smart enough. Even in those skills where we do best, we will never be perfect. God is *almighty*. He can do everything perfectly and without effort.

However hard we study, most knowledge will never be ours in this life. God is *all-knowing*. He knows all the mysteries of the universe and everything about himself. And unlike people, who can only think of one thing at a time, God can ''see'' all his knowledge at once.

We are always changing. We are for ever stopping one action and starting another. For example, we must often stop what we are doing and eat or go to sleep. We must move around after a long period of sitting or standing if we want to avoid getting cramps. Even growing, a change that is good for us, means leaving behind some of the joys of childhood in exchange for certain advantages of being grown up. How much better it would be to have the best things of childhood and adulthood, all at once!

Unlike us, God is *eternal* and *unchanging*. He never had a beginning or point where he ''started up'', nor will he ever come to an end. Nothing he does starts or stops either. He does not go from one joy to another, but enjoys all happiness eternally.

We cannot see God, because he is pure spirit; he has no body. Therefore he is not confined to one place at a time. God is *omnipresent*, meaning that he is everywhere.

Three in One

There is something else that may help us see that God couldn't have been "lonely" before he created the world. You have heard of it before. It is the Blessed Trinity.

Although there is only one God, there are three Persons in God: God the Father, God the Son, and God the Holy Spirit. From all eternity, the Father, Son, and Holy Spirit knew and loved one another. Each of the three Persons has all the perfections of God we have discussed.

The Blessed Trinity is a mystery we will never completely understand, even in Heaven. When we think of the Trinity now, we usually make the mistake of picturing three gods, not one, or of picturing one God with three "parts". Neither is correct. There is only one God, yet each of the three divine Persons is completely God, not one-third of God. The Church's teachers describe this by saying that although there are three *Persons* in God, he has only one *nature*.

By *nature* we mean *what* a thing is. Person means *who* someone is. Suppose you ran into a friendly alien from another planet who had just landed on earth. If he asked: "What are you?" your answer would be "a human being". If he then asked "Who are you?" you would reply, "Sarah", "John", or whatever your name is. With the Blessed Trinity, the answer to "What are you?" would be "God". The answer to "Who are you?" would be "God the Father, God the Son, and God the Holy Spirit."

This Is a Mystery

You may wonder why we bother studying something that we cannot really understand. The reason is that God wants us to know as much about him as we can. Otherwise, he would not have told us about himself. Also, if we love someone, we want to know things about that person. We love to hear our parents tell us about their childhood. We are happy to learn even a little about our Heavenly Father. We look forward to learning much more when we finally come to live with him in Heaven.

Words to Know:

> Trinity   nature   Person

> I arise today
> Through a mighty strength,
> The invocation of the Trinity.
> Through belief in the threeness,
> Through confession of the oneness,
> Of the Creator of creation
>
> — St. Patrick

"I believe in God, the Father almighty. . . , in Jesus Christ, his only Son Our Lord. . . , and in the Holy Spirit. . . ."

14

Q. 8 *What does "Unity of God" mean?*

By "Unity of God" we mean that there is only one God.

Q. 9 *What does "Trinity of God" mean?*

By "Trinity of God" we mean that there are three equal persons in God, really distinct from each other: the Father, the Son, and the Holy Spirit.

Q. 10 *What does "three Persons really distinct" mean?*

By "three Persons really distinct" we mean that in God one Person is not the other Person, although at the same time all three are one God.

Q. 11 *Do we understand how the three Divine Persons, although really distinct, are only one God?*

We do not understand nor can we understand how the three Divine Persons, although really distinct, are only one God. This is a mystery.

Q. 12 *Who is the first Person of the Most Holy Trinity?*
The first Person of the Most Holy Trinity is the *Father*.

Q. 13 *Who is the second Person of the Most Holy Trinity?*
The second Person of the Most Holy Trinity is the *Son*.

Q. 14 *Who is the third Person of the Most Holy Trinity?*
The third Person of the Most Holy Trinity is the *Holy Spirit*.

Q. 15 *Why is the Father the first Person of the Most Holy Trinity?*
The Father is the first Person of the Most Holy Trinity because he does not proceed from another Person and because the other two Persons, the Son and the Holy Spirit, proceed from him.

Q. 16 *Why is the Son the second Person of the Holy Trinity?*
The Son is the second Person of the Holy Trinity because he is generated by the Father and because he together with the Father is the principle of the Holy Spirit.

Q. 17 *Why is the Holy Spirit the third Person of the Most Holy Trinity?*
The Holy Spirit is the third Person of the Most Holy Trinity because he proceeds from the Father and the Son.

Q. 18 *Is each Person of the Most Holy Trinity God?*
Yes, each Person of the Most Holy Trinity is God.

Q. 19 *If each Divine Person is God, are the three Divine Persons therefore three gods?*
The three Divine Persons are not three gods, but only one God, because they have the one and same *unique* divine nature or substance.

Q. 20 *Are the three Divine Persons equal, or is one greater, more powerful, and more wise than the others?*

The three Divine persons, since they are only one God, are equal in every respect, and they possess equally and in common every perfection and every action. However, certain perfections and certain things that they do are attributed more to one Person than to another, as, for example, divine power and the activity of creation are attributed to the Father.

Q. 21 *But at least the Father existed before the Son and the Holy Spirit, did he not?*

The Father did not exist before the Son and the Holy Spirit, because the three Divine Persons, having in common the unique divine nature which is eternal, are all equally eternal.

CHAPTER 3

Creator of Heaven And Earth

Create, Creator, creation, creature: all of these words go together. They tell us about God, the universe, and ourselves.

God is the Creator of Heaven and earth. This means that he made everything. A man may say he has "created" a work of art or a line of fashion clothing. But he did not create them out of nothing. He used things that were already around, such as paint or cloth. Only God can truly create. That is, only God can bring something into being from nothing.

All that God has made we call "creation". That includes both Heaven and earth. Each thing that God has created is a "creature". (You can see the same root word in "create" and "creature".) "Creature" usually brings to mind a lizard, a spider, or something out of a science fiction movie. But an angel is just as much a creature as a lizard—or a mountain or a star or a man.

Is God a creature? Of course not! God alone is uncreated. He had no beginning. God is the cause of all creation. A fairy tale is not written by a fairy-tale character, but by someone who is outside of the story. In a similar way, God is not "part" of creation.

As we learned in the last chapter, God did not need to create Heaven and earth. But in his wisdom, he "saw that it was good" (Gen 1).

And in his love, he wanted others to enjoy the gift of life. He wanted to give others the chance to know and love him. Not only God the Father but God the Son and God the Holy Spirit took part in creation. We learn this from the Bible. "The Spirit of God moved across the waters", we read in the story of creation (Gen 1:3). And when speaking of Jesus, God's Son, Saint John's Gospel says, "All things were made through him" (Jn 1:3).

Most people believe in God through faith. But if we take a look at creation and think carefully, our minds can discover many things about God. First, we can learn that there *is* a God. How could this world have come to be without him? Some people do not believe in God. They think the universe made itself when mindless atoms came together by chance to make the stars and planets. But we know that nothing can make itself. The parts of a computer do not just come together by themselves. Paint dripping on paper does not make itself into a picture of a mountain scene or a field of flowers. It takes an intelligent mind to build a computer or paint a picture. The universe is even more complicated and beautiful. Only the perfect mind of God could have designed it.

Not only did God create the world, but he keeps it going according to his plan. You can see how plants, animals, minerals, and the weather seem to work together in harmony. Yet we know they do not think about working together. The earth does not say, ''I should turn on my axis so that there can be day and night.'' The squirrel does not think to himself, ''It is a good thing I forget to dig up some of the acorns I bury. They will grow into oak trees someday.'' Like the wise and loving father of many children, God directs all his creatures.

Many people, especially adults, do not stop to admire the things God has created or to thank him for them. Knowing that God made the world—and made it for us—should make us see the world in a new light. God made Heaven and earth for you. They exist to remind you of God and to show you how great and good he is. He wants you to enjoy them and be grateful for them.

Next time you visit a zoo or see a wildlife program on TV think about God. Remember that he made monkeys, raccoons, and bear cubs funny and entertaining for a reason. The reason is that he knew you would enjoy them that way.

God knows that even little things, like the first snow of winter or the first robin of spring, can give us joy. That is partly why he made them. God is the Father of all creation and the loving Father of each of us. He made the world for you.

God has given us rule over a part of creation so we may make a right and wise use of it. That is why it is wrong for us to abuse or waste any of God's creation and gift to us.

Words to Know:

create

Q. 22 *Why is God called ''the Creator of Heaven and earth''?*
God is called the Creator of Heaven and earth, that is, of the whole world, because he made it out of nothing. Making something out of nothing is to create.

Q. 23 *Is the world entirely the work of God?*
Yes, the world is entirely the work of God; and in its wonderful greatness, beauty, and order, it reflects to us the infinite power, wisdom, and goodness of God.

Q. 24 *Did God create only the matter that is in the world?*
No, God did not create only the material things that are in the world, but he created also the pure spirits, and he creates the soul of each human being.

The Beauty of Creation Bears Witness to God

Question the beauty of the earth,
the beauty of the sea,
the beauty of the wide air around you,
the beauty of the sky;
question the order of the stars,
the sun whose brightness lights the day,
the moon whose splendor softens the gloom of night;
question the living creatures that move in the waters,
that roam upon the earth,
that fly through the air;
the spirit that lies hidden,
the matter that is manifest;
the visible things that are ruled,
the invisible things that rule them;
question all these.
They will answer you:
"Behold and see, we are beautiful."
Their beauty is their confession of God.
Who made these beautiful changing things,
if not one who is beautiful and changeth not?

— St. Augustine

"I believe in God . . . the Creator of Heaven and earth"

CHAPTER 4

Realm of the Angels

There have been plenty of stories and movies about visitors from outer space. Advertisements for them often include such statements as "We are not alone." This is supposed to mean that the people of planet Earth are not the only intelligent creatures in the universe.

Whatever anyone thinks about creatures from Mars in flying saucers, it is indeed true that we are not alone. There really are creatures, not human beings, with intelligence watching you right now!

There is no use looking over your shoulder. These beings, God's angels, are ordinarily invisible to our eyes. It is by faith that we know angels exist and are a part of God's creation. They have no bodies. Like God they are pure spirits. They move and act by using their minds. That is why angels are pictured with wings. They can go where they want as quick as a thought, just by wanting to be there.

Angels in a picture might all look the same: long rows of figures in white robes. But every angel is different. Church tradition tells us that there are different groups or "orders" of angels. You have heard of *cherubim* and *seraphim* in the Preface of the Mass and in the song "Hail Holy Queen". These are two orders of angels. In the Bible we learn of another order, called *archangels*. Saint Gabriel is one of these. Some angels have greater power and intelligence than others, but all are superior to men. Even the "lowest" angel knows more than all the wise men who have ever lived.

According to Tradition, after God created the angels, he tested them. We do not know what the test was. The angels who loved God and wanted to serve him passed the test. They were welcomed into Heaven. Other angels refused to serve God. They admired their own perfections too much, and they refused to serve God as Lord of all. One of them had been the highest of all the angels, Lucifer. When Lucifer (who is now called Satan) rejected God, he and his followers became demons. They had to leave God's presence and never return. Ever since then they have hated God and tried to make others hate him too.

The word angel means "messenger". We often find angels in the Bible acting as God's messengers, bringing to people news of God's plan for them. The story that first comes to mind is that of the angel Gabriel. He brought to Mary the good news that God had chosen her to be the Mother of the Savior. In the Old Testament three angels visited Abraham, appearing and acting like men. They told Abraham that his old and childless wife, Sarah, would have a son that year. In the book of Tobit, the archangel Raphael takes the appearance of a young man. He guides young Tobias on a long journey to recover a debt owed to his parents.

On this journey he leads Tobias to his future wife and gives him the means of curing his father's blindness.

Other examples of the angel's work can be found in the Gospels. Angels announced the good news of Jesus' birth to the shepherds. Angels came to care for Jesus after he had fasted forty days and been tempted by the devil.

Angels, both good and bad, are more active in our world than we may think. Satan and the bad angels would rather have us think they were not around, but they are. They are miserably unhappy and they want to see us unhappy too by drawing us away from God, our true source of happiness.

On the other hand, God has given each of us a guardian angel. Our guardian angels inspire us to do what is good. They show us what God wants us to do. Guardian angels protect us not only from danger to our souls but danger to our bodies as well. You may have had some close escapes from death or serious injury. It is often your angel who helps you at these times.

Why not get to know your guardian angel better? Talk to him. Ask for his help when you are lonely, afraid, or tempted to sin. Pray to your guardian angel each day.

Angels are splendid creatures; very powerful and very intelligent. They are the friends and servants of God, and we owe them reverence and respect, almost in the same way as we owe it to a teacher or parent or older person. We should be especially grateful to our guardian angel who watches over us.

A chapter on angels would not be complete without mentioning Saint Michael the Archangel. Scripture and Tradition tell us that Michael was captain of the good angels who drove Lucifer and the bad angels out of Heaven. The Church calls upon Saint Michael to defend her in the battle against evil. Paintings of Saint Michael show him with a sword or spear, standing over Satan in victory. With the help of the angels we too can overcome sin.

Words to Know:

pure spirit   angel   demon

PRAYER TO ST. MICHAEL

St. Michael, the Archangel, defend us in battle. Be our protection against the wickedness and snares of the devil. May God rebuke him, we humbly pray, and do thou, O prince of the heavenly hosts, by the power of God, thrust into Hell Satan and the other evil spirits who prowl about the world seeking the ruin of souls. *Amen.*

Become familiar with the angels; for without being seen, they are present with you. Pray often to them, praise them constantly, and use their aid and assistance in all your affairs.

— St. Francis de Sales

"For he will give his angels charge of you to guard you in all your ways."

(Psalm 91:11)

Q. 25 *What are the pure spirits?*

The pure spirits are intelligent beings that do not have a body.

Q. 26 *How do we know that creatures which are pure spirits exist?*

That there are creatures which are pure spirits is known to us by faith.

Q. 27 *What creatures that are pure spirits do we know through faith?*

Through faith we know that there are pure spirits which are good, namely, the angels, and pure spirits which are wicked, the demons.

Q. 28 *What are the angels?*

The angels are invisible ministers of God, and they are also our guardians, for God has entrusted each man to one of these guardian angels.

Q. 29 *Do we have duties toward the angels?*

We have the duty of reverence and respect toward the angels; and toward our guardian angel we also have the duty of gratitude, of giving ear to his inspirations, and of never offending his presence by sin.

Q. 30 *What are the demons?*

The demons are angels who rebelled against God by pride and were cast into Hell; through their hatred of God, they tempt man to do evil.

CHAPTER 5

Made in His Image

Of all God's creatures, none is more unusual than man. Only man shares both the world of the angels and the world of the animals. Since man is made up of body and soul he is part of the spiritual order with the angels and part of the material order with the animals and plants. Because of his soul man can think, know, and freely choose what is good or evil. A man's soul will never die; it is immortal. As you know animals do not have the kind of souls that live for ever. Nor can they think or choose.

On the other hand, because he has a body man shares with the animals some things that angels do not have. He can feel things, he has the senses of sight, hearing, touch, taste, and smell. He needs air, food, and water to stay alive.

To understand better the wonderful mystery of ourselves, we must know about the first man and woman. All of the rest of us have descended from them; that is why we call them our first parents.

God made Adam and Eve as he wanted them to be. They had all they needed physically and mentally to live lives of happiness according to his will. They were given special gifts so that living in the Garden of Eden was without hardship or difficulty; they would never be sick, would never suffer, and they would not have to die. Their wills were not weak as ours are, and they saw and understood things clearly.

Before original sin, all these perfections were part of what it meant to be human. But God also gave our first parents a gift that was supernatural. God gave Adam and Eve a share of his own life, the life of grace. This means that after enjoying life on earth for a while, Adam and Eve could enjoy being with God in Heaven. There would be no death in between this world and Heaven. This gift was not only for Adam and Eve, but for all their descendants, ourselves included.

The Bible tells us that when God created Adam, he said, "Let us make man in our own image." This does not mean that God has a body like us. It means that we are like God in our minds and in our freedom to choose. God loves each of us as his children. Because of this, each of us has great worth and value. It makes no difference if someone is badly handicapped, retarded, or unloved by other people. Even a tiny unborn baby growing within its mother is more important than all the stars in the sky, all the inventions of science, and all the works of art. Each of us is known and loved by God. That is what matters more than anything else.

Words to Know:

soul   free will   grace

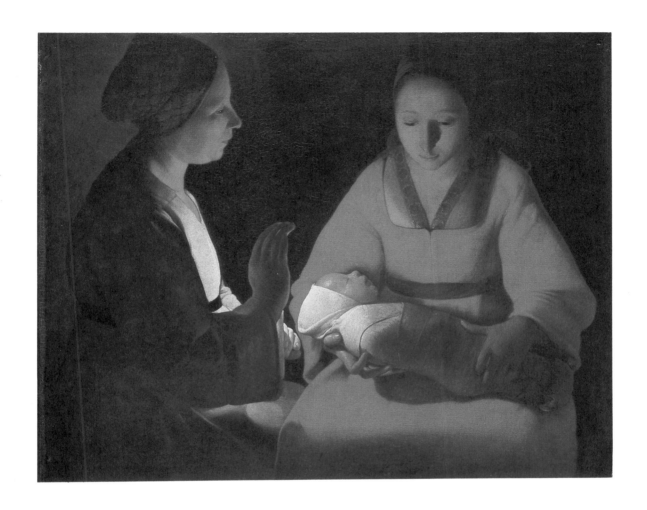

"What is man that you should be mindful of him, the son of man that you should care for him? You have made him little less than the angels and crowned him with glory and honor. You have given him rule over the works of your hands, putting all things under his feet."

(Psalm 8:5—7)

Q. 31 *What is man?*

Man is a reasoning being, composed of body and soul.

Q. 32 *What is the soul?*

The soul is the spiritual part of man, by which he lives, understands, and is free; hence he is able to know, love, and serve God.

Q. 33 *Does man's soul die with his body?*

Man's soul does not die with his body, but it lives for ever because it is a spiritual reality.

Q. 34 *What care must we take of our soul?*

We must take the greatest care of our soul because it is our better part, because it is immortal, and because only by saving our soul can we be happy for ever.

Q. 35 *Who were the first men?*

The first men were Adam and Eve, who were created immediately by God. All other men descend from them. Hence they are called our *first parents*.

Q. 36 *Was man created weak and sinful as we are now?*

Man was not created weak and sinful as we are now, but in a state of happiness, with a destiny and with gifts that were above the capacity of human nature.

Q. 37 *What destiny did God assign to man?*

God assigned to man the supreme destiny of seeing and enjoying him, the Infinite Good, for ever. And because this is entirely above and beyond the capacity of human nature, man also received from God a supernatural power to achieve this destiny. This power is called *grace*.

CHAPTER 6

The Fall from Grace

God gave Adam and Eve a life free from pain, sickness, or death. They lived in harmony with all living things on earth. With the gift of sanctifying grace, they knew God as a friend and were confident of eternal life with him.

As with the angels, God tested Adam and Eve. He gave them the chance to show their love and thanks for all he had given them. All they had to do was freely obey God's command. And they had been carefully warned that disobedience would have terrible consequences.

Adam and Eve did not pass the test. Satan tempted Eve with the same desire for power that ruined him: ''You shall be like gods.'' Eve rejected the happiness God had given her and believed the lies of Satan. She was guilty of tremendous pride as well as disobedience. Eve's next action was far from god-like. She convinced Adam to disobey God along with her.

With Adam's act of disobedience God's grace left the souls of Adam and Eve. They had great feelings of guilt and shame. Adam and Eve tried to hide from God. They must have known that this was impossible, but that is what sin makes us wish to do. Even when God spoke to them, they were not sensible enough to confess their sin and ask God's forgiveness. Instead they tried to put the blame somewhere else: ''Eve told me to do it.'' ''The serpent tempted me.''

It sounds familiar, doesn't it? ''He hit me first.'' ''It's not my fault. She broke my pencil.'' It is not a coincidence that we behave like Adam and Eve when we have done something wrong. By sinning, Adam hurt not only himself. Having lost God's gifts, he could not pass them on to his children. Just as some people pass on defects to their children, Adam

passed on *original sin* to us. It is called original sin because it was committed at the beginning of the human race, and it is passed on to each of us at our own beginning. Someone might think that it is unjust of God to punish all of us for Adam's sin. But we must remember that what Adam and Eve lost because of original sin were free gifts which God had given them. The life of grace is something to which none of us has a right.

The effects of original sin include a strong inclination to sin. In simpler words, it is easy for us to sin. Our minds cannot control our feelings very easily. Even when we want very much to be good, we often give in to sin anyway. That is why some people say it was "unfair" of God to punish Adam and Eve for one sin. They forget that before original sin, Adam and Eve were not like us. They were in control of their feelings. With sanctifying grace and their great knowledge, they did not really "feel like" doing evil the way we do. That is why the first sin was so serious and deserved such great punishment.

After sinning, Adam and Eve had to leave Paradise and raise their children in a world of pain, exhausting work, and ignorance. They and their descendants would end their time on earth with death. There was no hope of eternal life in Heaven by their own efforts.

But God loved his children too much to abandon them. He promised to send his Son to earth to be the New Adam, the perfect man who would "pass the test" on behalf of all men. Jesus would obediently accept death on a Cross to make up for the sin of Adam and for all sins committed since then. His death would open Heaven to all who had died (like Adam and Eve) hoping in God's mercy. The sacrament of Baptism brings the graces of Christ's death to each of us. Baptism removes original sin, fills our souls with sanctifying grace, and makes us God's children.

In the next few chapters we will see how God helped his people through the thousands of years before Christ's coming. We will see how he prepared the entire world for the Good News of salvation.

Pain and Suffering

Throughout history, man has wondered why there is pain and suffering in the world. All suffering is in some way the result of sin. It is easy to see, for instance, that the pain and sorrow caused by war, murder, hatred, anger, and greed is very much "man-made". But what about earthquakes, floods, and terrible diseases?

Before original sin, man was in control of the natural world. The human body was stronger than any of the tiny organisms that cause sickness. God had given mankind a home that was free from natural disaster. The sin of Adam did more than weaken our souls with the loss of sanctifying grace. In some ways it threw all of nature out of balance, too. That is why we can say that the suffering which comes from the natural world is also the result of sin.

It is sometimes hard to see why God allows so much suffering to go on. But we have to trust that he has a reason. After all, he has shown us his love in many ways, especially by sending his own Son to endure horrible pain in order to save us. God can always bring good out of suffering. It is a bad thing for a man to lose all his money, but this may teach that man to turn to God in prayer for the first time in his life. It seems cruel and unjust when a baby dies in an accident before it can grow up and enjoy life. But perhaps that baby might never have reached Heaven if it had grown up and turned to a life of sin. Only God knows the reason for the suffering that comes to each of us in this life. But in Heaven he will answer all the questions we may have about it.

"The man and his wife hid themselves from the presence of the Lord God among the trees of the garden."

(Genesis 3:8)

Q. 38 *What was Adam's sin?*

Adam's sin was a grave sin of pride and disobedience.

Q. 39 *What damage did the sin of Adam cause?*

The sin of Adam despoiled him and all men of grace and of every other supernatural gift. Thus Adam and all men were made subject to sin, to the demon, to death, to ignorance, to all evil inclinations, and to every other sort of misery, and finally to exclusion from Heaven.

Q. 40 *What is the sin called to which Adam subjected the rest of men by his fault?*

The sin to which Adam subjected all men with his fault is called the *original sin* because it was committed at the origin of mankind and is transmitted with human nature to each and every man in his own origin.

Q. 41 *In what does original sin consist?*

Original sin consists in the privation of the original grace, which God intended us to have, but which we do not have because the head of mankind with his disobedience deprived himself and all of us who descend from him of this grace.

Q. 42 *Is God unjust in punishing us on account of the sin of Adam?*

God is not unjust in punishing us on account of the sin of Adam, because original sin does not take away from us anything to which we have a strict right as human beings, but only the free gifts which God in his goodness would have bestowed on us if Adam had not sinned.

Q. 43 *Because of original sin, did man have to remain excluded for ever from Heaven?*

Because of original sin, man would have had to remain excluded for ever from Heaven, if God had not promised and sent his own Son, Jesus Christ, from Heaven to save mankind.

CHAPTER 7

The Chosen People

Many years passed since the time of Adam and Eve. What men had once known about God had been forgotten by most. They worshipped false gods or perhaps none at all. They had forgotten about God's promise to send a Savior. In order to keep knowledge and love of the true God among men, God chose a special group of people who would have faith in him and receive his special care and attention. This chosen group would be the channel through which God would prepare the world for the promised Messiah. It would be these people who would keep alive God's promise to free the human race from sin and lead it to salvation. God chose Abraham to be the father of this chosen people.

Few people in history have had faith like that of Abraham. When God asked him to leave his hometown of Ur, Abraham took his wife, Sarah, and did so at once. He settled in the unfamiliar land of Canaan simply because God told him to. He believed God's promise that his descendants would be more numerous than the stars, despite the fact that Sarah was too old to have children. God rewarded Abraham's faith with the birth of a son, Isaac.

Then God told Abraham to offer Isaac as a sacrifice. It must have been a terrible decision for Abraham to make. On the one hand, Abraham loved and trusted God. On the other hand, the thought of killing his little boy must have been almost more than Abraham could bear. And he must have wondered what God meant, promising him numerous descendants, then asking him to put an end to the only descendant he had. Yet Abraham chose to act in obedience to God's command, still having faith and believing that somehow his descendants would be numerous. God sent an angel to stop Abraham at the last minute, and let him know how pleased God was:

I swear by myself, declares the Lord, that because you acted as you did in not withholding from me your beloved son, I will bless you abundantly and make your descendants as countless as the stars of the sky and the sands of the seashore;

> "By faith Abraham, when he was tested, offered up Isaac, and he who had received the promises was ready to offer up his only son, of whom it was said, 'Through Isaac shall your descendants be named.' He considered that God was able to raise men even from the dead; hence . . . he did receive him back."
>
> (Hebrews 11:17−19)

your descendants shall take possession of the gates of their enemies, and in your descendants all the nations of the earth shall find blessing—all this because you obeyed my command. (Gen 22:16−18)

***

Isaac grew up; he married Rebecca, and they had twin sons, Esau and Jacob. Esau was considered the eldest because he was born slightly before Jacob. He was Isaac's favorite—strong and athletic. Jacob was loved best by Rebecca. He was gentle and home loving. Rebecca had received from God a prophecy that Jacob, although the younger of the two, would be greater than Esau. "And the older shall serve the younger" (Gen 25:23).

As the two grew up, the prophecy certainly seemed to be coming true. One day, Esau came home after a long hunting trip, weak with hunger. Jacob was cooking a stew. "You must give me something to eat, Jacob," he said, "I'm starving." "Not unless you promise to give me your rights and inheritance as first-born", said Jacob. Esau agreed.

Later, Jacob obtained from his father a special blessing that was really meant for Esau.

Esau was furious and threatened to kill his brother. Rebecca told Jacob to leave home until Esau's anger passed.

During his time away from home, Jacob married and was blessed with twelve sons. From these twelve sons descended the twelve tribes of Israel. (God later changed Jacob's name to Israel. That is why the chosen people were known as the Israelites.) One of the twelve, Joseph, was sold into slavery in Egypt by his jealous brothers. But God brought good out of the brothers' sin. He used Joseph to save his family from famine. As you may recall, Joseph interpreted the dreams of Pharaoh, the Egyptian ruler, predicting that seven years of good harvest would be followed by seven years of famine. Pharaoh put Joseph in charge of storing enough grain during the good years to feed the people when the bad years came. When the years of famine arrived, Joseph's brothers came to Egypt. They were happily reunited with their long lost brother, who forgave them all. Jacob and all his sons settled in Egypt and raised their families. God's promise to Abraham was carried out in Isaac, Jacob, and Jacob's twelve sons. God's chosen people, the people who would prepare the world for salvation, were becoming numerous indeed.

CHAPTER 8

Moses Leads God's People

Years passed, and a new Pharaoh came into power. The Egyptians forgot how their ancestors were saved from starvation by Joseph. Now they looked upon the Hebrew people with resentment. "Why do these people refuse to worship our gods? And what do they mean by having so many children? Perhaps they plan to outnumber us and take over Egypt!"

Such thoughts prompted Pharaoh to enslave the Israelites. He forced them to labor from morning until night, building the roads and cities of Egypt. Then he decreed that all baby boys born to the Israelites must be killed.

One young Hebrew mother kept her infant son hidden for three months. She knew she could not do this much longer before the Egyptians found out, so she placed the child in a large, waterproof basket. The basket was placed among the reeds on the shore of the Nile River. The baby's older sister, Miriam, watched from a distance to see what would happen.

What happened shows that not only the mother, but God himself, had a special reason for wanting this baby to live. The Pharaoh's daughter came along and discovered the basket. She was delighted to find a tiny baby inside and decided to adopt him as her own. Miriam saw all this and decided to act. She knew that wealthy women always had slaves to nurse their babies. Miriam came out of hiding, and offered to find a Hebrew woman for this job.

Naturally, she brought the baby's own mother. Pharaoh's daughter named the child Moses, which means "drawn from the water".

Moses grew up in the palace of Pharaoh. As he grew older, he was disturbed at the way his people were treated. One day Moses saw an Egyptian beating a Hebrew slave. Unable to stand such injustice any longer, Moses rushed forward and killed the Egyptian. Soon word of what Moses had done got around, and he began to fear for his life. He fled from Egypt and settled in the land of Midian. Here he married and became a herdsman.

Perhaps Moses thought he was through with Egypt. But God was not through with Moses. One day, as Moses tended his flock, he saw a flaming bush that was not consumed by the fire. From the bush came the voice of God calling out to him and saying:

I am the God of your father, the God of Abraham, the God of Isaac, and the God of Jacob. . . .

I have seen the affliction of my people who are in Egypt and have heard their cry because of their taskmasters; I know their sufferings, and I have come down to deliver them out of the hand of the Egyptians. . . . Come, I will send you to Pharaoh that you may bring forth my people. . . . (Ex 3:6—10)

The cry of the people of Israel has

come to me and I have seen the oppression with which the Egyptians oppress them. Come, I will send you to Pharaoh that you may bring forth my people, the sons of Israel, out of Egypt. (Ex 3:9—10)

At first, Moses answered God, not with faith, but excuses: Who am I to do such a great thing? What shall I tell people when they ask your Name? No one will believe me when I say that you sent me. I am not a good public speaker, Lord; you had better send someone else. But God answered all these questions. He gave Moses the power to perform miracles that would prove his claim. He told Moses his Name: "I AM". God told Moses to have his brother Aaron speak for him.

So Moses returned to Egypt with Aaron and they went before Pharaoh demanding that Pharaoh let the Israelites go. Of course, Pharaoh would not hear of releasing the Israelites. Because of Pharaoh's disbelief and refusal, God brought through Moses ten punishments or plagues upon Egypt as a sign of his power and dominion. First, Moses struck the waters of the Nile with his staff, and all the water of Egypt turned to blood. But Pharaoh did not change his mind. Plagues that followed included invasions of frogs and gnats, a disease that killed many cattle, painful boils, hail, locusts that devoured crops, and darkness over the land. Pharaoh's heart remained hardened, as Scripture tells us, so God had to send the worst plague of all. Moses warned Pharaoh that if he did not let God's chosen people go, every firstborn in Egypt, of man and animal alike, would die that night. Pharaoh still did not listen.

The First Passover and Freedom for Israel

Meanwhile, God had given Moses special instructions, both to save the Israelites from the plague which would kill the firstborn, and to get the people ready to leave Egypt. Each family was to slaughter a lamb, then mark its door with the lamb's blood. Seeing the bloodstain, the angel of death would pass by that house. The family was to roast the lamb and eat it with bitter herbs and bread. The women were told to make the bread without yeast (unleavened), because they would not have time to let it rise. The Israelites were to eat this dinner standing and dressed for travel. This night is remembered every year even in our time, as Jews the world over celebrate the feast of Passover.

The plague came, and all the firstborn of the Egyptians died, including Pharaoh's son. At last Pharaoh told Moses to take the Hebrews and leave Egypt. However, they had only gone a day's journey when Pharaoh changed his mind. He sent his armies out to recapture the Hebrews. Moses and his people had just reached the shores of the Red Sea. It seemed as if they were trapped.

But instead, God gave his chosen people a great sign of his power and love. In answer to the prayers of Moses, he caused the waters to separate. The Israelites passed through on dry ground. When Pharaoh's armies entered the Red Sea, the waters rushed back, destroying them all. Moses and the people sang in praise of God: "I will sing to the Lord, for he is gloriously triumphant; horse and rider he has thrown into the sea" (Ex 15:1).

God led his people on through the desert. It was a difficult journey. But God was with them, caring for all their needs and protecting them from dangers, and willing to forgive them whenever they complained or sinned against him.

Words to Know:

Passover

36

Symbols of Salvation

The story of Moses and the escape from Egypt are true history. But in his wisdom, God also used these events to stand for, or "prefigure", the mystery of our redemption by Jesus Christ.

The captivity of the Israelites in Egypt symbolizes the captivity of the human race to sin. Just as the Israelites needed God's special intervention to free them, so, too, did mankind need a Savior from God in order to be freed from sin.

The blood of the lamb on the doors saved the Hebrews from the angel of death. Jesus shed *his* blood to save us from the death of sin. This is why one prayer at Mass calls Jesus the "Lamb of God".

The Israelites passed through the Red Sea into freedom. Those same waters destroyed the evil armies of Pharaoh. In Baptism we pass through water into a new life of grace. The evil of original sin is destroyed by the baptismal waters.

O give thanks to the Lord, call on his name,
  make known his deeds among the peoples!
Sing to him, sing praises to him,
  tell of all his wonderful works!
Glory in his holy name; let the hearts of those
  who seek the Lord rejoice!
Seek the Lord and his strength,
  seek his presence continually!
Remember the wonderful works that he has done,
  his miracles, and the judgments he uttered,
O offspring of Abraham his servant,
  sons of Jacob, his chosen ones!

He is the Lord our God;
  his judgments are in all the earth.
He is mindful of his covenant for ever,
  of the word that he commanded,
  for a thousand generations,
the covenant which he made with Abraham,
  his sworn promise to Isaac,
which he confirmed to Jacob as a statute,
  to Israel as an everlasting covenant,
saying, "To you I will give the land of Canaan
  as your portion for an inheritance."

When they were few in number,
  of little account, and sojourners in it,
wandering from nation to nation,
  from one kingdom to another people,
he allowed no one to oppress them;
  he rebuked kings on their account,
saying, "Touch not my anointed ones,
  do my prophets no harm!"

When he summoned a famine on the land,
  and broke every staff of bread,
he had sent a man ahead of them,
  Joseph, who was sold as a slave.
His feet were hurt with fetters,
  his neck was put in a collar of iron;
until what he had said came to pass
  the word of the Lord tested him.
The king sent and released him,
  the ruler of the peoples set him free;
he made him lord of his house,
  and ruler of all his possessions,
to instruct his princes at his pleasure
  and to teach his elders wisdom.

Then Israel came to Egypt;
  Jacob sojourned in the land of Ham.

And the Lord made his people very fruitful,
  and made them stronger than their foes.
He turned their hearts to hate his people,
  to deal craftily with his servants.

He sent Moses his servant,
  and Aaron whom he had chosen.
They wrought his signs among them,
  and miracles in the land of Ham.
He sent darkness, and made the land dark;
  they rebelled against his words.
He turned their waters into blood,
  and caused their fish to die.
Their land swarmed with frogs,
  even in the chambers of their kings.
He spoke, and there came swarms of flies,
  and gnats throughout their country.
He gave them hail for rain,
  and lightning that flashed through their land.
He smote their vines and fig trees,
  and shattered the trees of their country.
He spoke, and the locusts came,
  and young locusts without number;
which devoured all the vegetation in their land,
  and ate up the fruit of their ground.
He smote all the first-born in their land,
  the first issue of all their strength.

Then he led forth Israel with silver and gold,
  and there was none among his tribes who stumbled.
Egypt was glad when they departed,
  for dread of them had fallen upon it.
He spread a cloud for a covering,
  and fire to give light by night.
They asked, and he brought quails, and gave
  them bread from heaven in abundance.
He opened the rock, and water gushed forth;
  it flowed through the desert like a river.
For he remembered his holy promise,
  and Abraham his servant.

So he led forth his people with joy,
  his chosen ones with singing,
And he gave them the lands of the nations;
  and they took possession of the fruit of the
    peoples' toil,
to the end that they should keep his statutes,
  and observe his laws.
Praise the Lord!

CHAPTER 9

The Forming of God's People

If you have a two- or three-year-old brother or sister at home, you have noticed how a child behaves when something goes wrong. When he cannot find a toy, he bursts into tears and wails, ''I can't find my truck.'' When a puzzle is too hard, he angrily throws it across the room. As much as babies love and trust their parents, they simply forget to ask them calmly for help. All they can think of is how impossible it is to solve a problem by themselves. For the moment, they do not remember that someone more powerful than themselves, who loves them very much, would be happy to help if asked.

This is how the chosen people often behaved as they wandered in the desert with Moses. Whenever they needed something, they would begin by complaining to Moses, instead of turning in prayer to God their Father. As soon as their food supplies from Egypt ran low, they cried, ''If only we had stayed in Egypt, where at least we had food to eat. Why have you brought us into this desert to die of starvation?'' (Ex 16:3).

Patient Father that he is, God showed his complaining children how much he cared for them. Each morning the ground was covered with flakes of a bread-like food. ''What is it?'' asked the people. The Hebrew word for

''What is it?'' is *manna* so that is how the food from Heaven got its name. Every evening, God sent flocks of quail to the Hebrew camp so the people could have meat for dinner.

One would think that after the miraculous appearance of manna and quail the people would have learned their lesson. But when they came to a place in the desert that had no water, the complaints began again. ''Moses, why did you make us leave Egypt, to kill our children and our animals with thirst?'' God instructed Moses to strike a rock with his staff. When he did, water came out of the rock.

But God wanted to do more for his chosen people than just give them food and drink. Since it was through this nation that salvation would be brought to all mankind they had to be special and set apart from all other people. And so God established a covenant with the Israelites to show that he would be their God and they would be his people. (Covenant means an agreement: God agreed to make the Hebrews his special children. The Hebrews agreed to follow the commandments.) He also gave other laws to guide the chosen people in their daily life.

But God wanted to do more for his chosen people than just give them food and drink. He also taught them how to live. He called Moses

up to Mount Sinai, forbidding the others to go near it. Covered by a cloud, Moses spent many days speaking with God. During this time God gave Moses the Ten Commandments. He also gave him other laws to guide the chosen people in their daily life.

God instructed Moses to have an "ark" or container made to hold the stone tablets on which the Ten Commandments were written. It was to be called the Ark of the Covenant. The Ark of the Covenant was to be the sign of God's presence among the Hebrews. It was to be the focal point of their prayer and worship.

Meanwhile, the Israelites grew restless while waiting for Moses. They were at the bottom of Mount Sinai offending God in a horrible way. They had made a golden calf and were wor-

shipping it as their god. They soon learned how much this angered God, not to mention Moses. In his mercy, God forgave those who were truly sorry and willing to follow Moses. In justice, he punished with death those who did not repent.

In the centuries that followed, the Israelites sinned against God many times. Often God had to punish them before they knew enough to be sorry and ask God's forgiveness. On the other hand, there were also many times when the chosen people trusted in God and obeyed his commands. God rewarded their obedience. He brought them into a land of plenty. He blessed them with large families. Most of all, through God's revelation they were the only nation on earth that had true knowledge and worship of the one true God.

Kings of Israel

As the years went by, the chosen people did not always like taking direction from God. They wanted to be like other nations. They asked God to appoint a king to rule over them. God warned the Hebrews that the rule of an earthly king would have disadvantages, but he allowed them to have a king just the same. So began the long line of kings that would govern the chosen people for many years. King David and his son, King Solomon, were the greatest of these kings. They did much to build up the nation of Israel. They saw to it that the people worshipped the one, true God. God promised David that from his descendants, would come the Savior, the eternal King whose rule would last for ever. Many of the kings that came after David were not good men. Some led the people into worship of false gods. But God kept his people in his special care, even through years of sin. He did not forget his promise that salvation of the world would come through them.

The Ten Commandments

1. I am the Lord your God; you shall not have strange gods before me.
2. You shall not take the Name of the Lord your God in vain.
3. Remember to keep holy the Lord's Day.
4. Honor your father and mother.
5. You shall not kill.
6. You shall not commit adultery.
7. You shall not steal.
8. You shall not bear false witness against your neighbor.
9. You shall not covet your neighbor's wife.
10. You shall not covet your neighbor's goods.

CHAPTER 10

The Words of the Prophets

When we hear the word "prophet", we usually think of someone who predicts the future. But foretelling the future was a small part of the Old Testament prophets' role. Their job was much more important than that. God called the prophets to keep the people of Israel from becoming just like other nations and to keep them mindful of their covenant with God.

How could that happen? Very simply. After the death of Solomon, the Hebrews were split in two. Some followed the successor of David, the others followed a different ruler. Both groups began forgetting about God and the commandments. Soon, they were worshipping false gods. Instead of remaining true to God after all he had done to make them a great nation, the Hebrews wanted to "be like everyone else". All the other tribes had gods of wood and stone, and the Hebrews did not want to be different. (That may sound silly, but all of us have at times done foolish things because we did not want to be different from our friends!) Before long, there was hardly any difference between the Hebrews and the pagan nations. Hebrews would even marry pagans. Without the faith and law that kept them a separate people from the world, the chosen people would simply blend in with other tribes until they no longer existed as a nation.

God kept this from happening by sending the prophets. The prophets reminded the people that they had broken their promises to God. He called on them to repent and change their lives. As you can imagine, the prophets were not always very popular. The Hebrews did not want to be told they were doing wrong. But when the Hebrews were defeated in war and taken into captivity, they realized they were being punished for their sins. They repented.

Isaiah

During the last centuries before the birth of Christ, the prophets also had to prepare the people for the coming of the Savior. Isaiah was one of those who made prophecies about the coming Messiah. He predicted that the Savior would be born of a virgin. He made it clear that he would be more than another earthly ruler:

His name shall be called Wonderful, Counselor, the Mighty God, the Everlasting Father, and Prince of Peace. (Isaiah 9:5−6)

The Jewish people were expecting a triumphant leader who would restore the kingdom of Israel. They must have been surprised when Isaiah spoke of the Savior's mission as one of pain and humiliation.

He was despised and rejected by men; a man of sorrows and acquainted with grief; and as one from whom men hide their faces he was despised, and we esteemed him not.

Surely he has borne our griefs and carried our sorrows; yet we esteemed him stricken, smitten by God, and afflicted. But he was wounded for our transgressions, he was bruised for our iniquities; upon him was the chastisement that made us whole, and with his stripes we were healed. (Is 53:3−5)

Jeremiah

The prophet Jeremiah came after Isaiah, at a time when the people had again fallen into idol worship. Jeremiah had to speak out against this and call the people to repentance. He had to oppose the sinful actions of the king of Israel. Because of this, Jeremiah suffered arrest and imprisonment on several occasions. Jeremiah predicted that the people would be punished for their sins, and it came to pass. There was famine, war, and finally captivity under the king of Babylon. During the captivity other prophets consoled the people with prophecies of the promised Messiah.

Other prophets followed Jeremiah. The last and greatest of the prophets began his mission, not before, but after the birth of Jesus. His name was Saint John the Baptist. You will learn more about him later.

Words to Know:

prophet

Some of the Prophets Whom God Sent to Israel

Elijah	Micah
Elisha	Nahum
Isaiah	Habakkuk
Jeremiah	Zephaniah
Ezekiel	Haggai
Hosea	Zechariah
Joel	Malachi
Amos	John the Baptist
Obadiah	

PART TWO

God the Son,
The Redeemer

CHAPTER 11

In the Fullness of Time

As we have seen, God kept his people waiting for the Savior for many centuries. In every generation he sent prophets and leaders to remind them of his promise and call them to reform their lives. We may wonder why God allowed so many people to live and die without seeing the Savior for whom they longed. We do not know why God chooses as he does. All we know is that in the fullness of time the Savior came.

During the days when Herod was king, a priest named Zachariah lived with his wife Elizabeth in the countryside of Judea. Like typical Jewish married couples, they wanted to have children. But sadly, they were unable to have any. Now they were so old they could no longer even hope for such a thing.

One day it was Zachariah's turn to offer incense to God in the Holy of Holies, the very holiest part of the Temple of Jerusalem. As he entered, the Archangel Gabriel appeared to him, saying: "Do not be afraid, Zachariah, your prayer has been heard. Your wife, Elizabeth, shall bear a son, whom you shall name John" (Lk 1:13). The angel explained that John would be no ordinary child but would grow up to be a great prophet and turn the hearts of many back to God.

But all this was too much for Zachariah. All he could think of was how impossible this seemed. "How am I to know this," he demanded. "I am an old man, my wife, too, is advanced in years." Since Zachariah answered without faith, the angel gave him a greater proof of God's power than he had bargained for: Zachariah would be unable to speak until the child was born! And so it was. When Zachariah staggered out from the Temple, he had to use signs and handwriting to tell people what had happened.

Six months passed by. As Elizabeth waited for the birth of her baby, Gabriel visited the earth again. This time he came to see Mary, the daughter of Anne and Joachim. Mary lived with her parents in the small town of Nazareth. "Hail, full of grace, the Lord is with you! Blessed are you among women!" Mary did not know what to make of the angel's words. The angel assured Mary that she had found great favor with God. "You will bear a son and call his name Jesus, for he shall save his people from their sins."

Mary was ready to do what God wanted, but she was not sure how. At the time she was not married, although she was engaged to a man named Joseph. Then the angel explained. "The Holy Spirit will come upon you and the power of the Most High will overshadow you, hence the holy offspring to be born shall be called the Son of God" (Lk 1:35).

Mary answered, "Behold the handmaid of the Lord, let it be done to me according to your word." Before the angel left, he told her about the baby that would soon be born to Elizabeth, her cousin. "Nothing is impossible with God", he said.

The angel left, and Mary immediately went to visit her cousin Elizabeth. The moment Elizabeth heard Mary's greeting the unborn child within her gave a tremendous leap. He seemed to be dancing with happiness! Elizabeth was filled with the Holy Spirit and said to Mary, "Blessed are you among women and blessed is the fruit of your womb. Who am I that the mother of my Lord should come to me?" (Lk 1:41—42).

Mary, in turn, was glad that Elizabeth shared her secret, and filled with joy at God's goodness. She burst into song:

My soul proclaims the greatness of the Lord,
my spirit rejoices in God my Savior
for he has looked with favor on his lowly
    servant.

From this day all generations will call me
    blessed:
the Almighty has done great things for me,
and holy is his name.

He has mercy on those who fear him
in every generation.

He has shown the strength of his arm;
He has scattered the proud in their conceit.

He has cast down the mighty from their thrones,
and has lifted up the lowly.

He has filled the hungry with good things, and
    the rich he has sent away empty.

He has come to the help of his servant Israel
for he has remembered his promise of mercy,
    the promise he made to our fathers,
to Abraham and his children for ever.

(Lk 1:46—55)

Mary stayed with Elizabeth about three months. When the baby was born, the relatives of Elizabeth and Zachariah came. They talked about a name for the baby. Elizabeth, knowing the message of the angel, insisted that the name John be given. Her relatives could not understand why. "You should name him Zachariah, after his father", they said. Finally they asked Zachariah for his decision. Taking a pen, he wrote, "His name is John." At that very moment, Zachariah had the power to speak again. He began to praise God and prophesy about little John's future:

Blessed be the Lord, the God of Israel;
he has come to his people and set them
free. . . . (Lk 1:68)

The son of Elizabeth and Zachariah grew up to be Saint John the Baptist, last of the prophets and herald of Jesus Christ.

Immaculate Conception

From the day the Angel Gabriel appeared to Mary, she knew her life would never be the same again. One day she was an unknown girl in the country village; the next day she was the Mother of the Savior her people had awaited for ages! And what is more, Mother of God's own Son!

The average girl might have been unable to handle so great a role. But Mary was no ordinary girl. God had prepared her to be the Mother of the Savior even before she was born. He had given her a great gift which we call Mary's Immaculate Conception.

As you have learned, we have all inherited original sin from our first parents. When Adam and Eve sinned they lost for themselves and for us the gift of sanctifying grace, God's life within the soul. Because of original sin we are weak and are easily tempted to sin. But God

48

preserved Mary from original sin. Her soul was filled with sanctifying grace from the moment of her conception. Mary had the power to do always what God wanted and never offend him by sin. Because God created Mary free from sin, she was worthy to become the Mother of Jesus.

The belief in the Immaculate Conception was held by the Church from its earliest days, but it was not proclaimed an official doctrine of the Church until December 8, 1854. Now we have a special Holy Day every year on December 8 to celebrate the gift of Mary's Immaculate Conception.

Words to Know:

Immaculate Conception
Annunciation   Magnificat

Father, we rejoice in the privilege of Our Lady's Immaculate Conception, which preserved her from the stain of sin by the power of Christ's redeeming death and prepared her to be the Mother of God. Grant that through her prayers we ourselves may come to you, cleansed from all sin. Through Christ Our Lord. *Amen*.

Q. 44 *Was anyone among the descendants of Adam ever preserved from original sin?*

Mary alone among the descendants of Adam has been preserved from original sin. Because she was chosen to be the Mother of God, she was "full of grace" (Lk 1:28), and hence free of sin from the first instant of her existence. For this reason the Church celebrates her *Immaculate Conception*.

CHAPTER 12

Born in the City of David

After Mary returned to Nazareth, Saint Joseph had a decision to make. Under Jewish law, he could not marry a woman who was going to have a baby. So Joseph decided to break his engagement with Mary quietly. But one night an angel came to him in a dream.

> Joseph, son of David, have no fear about taking Mary as your wife. It is by the Holy Spirit that she has conceived this child. She is to have a son, and you are to name him Jesus because he will save his people from their sins. (Mt 1:20—21)

Joseph was overjoyed that he would not have to break his engagement with Mary. He was even happier that the long-awaited Messiah, God's own Son, would be born into his family. The two were married, and settled down in Joseph's house in Nazareth.

The quiet life of the couple was disrupted by news that the Roman Emperor wished to take a census of the entire empire. This meant that Joseph and Mary would have to journey to Bethlehem, the town from which Joseph's family came. There Jesus was born, fulfilling the prophecy of Micah that the Savior would come from Bethlehem (Micah 5:1—4).

You have heard the Christmas story so often that there is no need to retell it here. But knowing a story too well can cause us to take it for granted. We are so used to the fact that God became one of us that we forget what a startling thing it is. Just think! The same God who created the blazing sun, who shaped the towering mountains, who looks upon the ocean as we might look upon a fish tank: this God came down from Heaven to share our life. This God of infinite beauty and power was born in a dark, smelly stable. Only his infinite love for us can explain God's desire to do this.

To see what it was like for God to become man, let us use our imaginations a bit. Imagine that you had to become some stupid, ugly creature while keeping your human intelligence —a snail, for example. Then suppose you had to teach the other snails about the world of humans: all the things we can do and the way we live. The catch is, you cannot speak "people talk" but only "snail talk", which does not have words for all the wonderful things people know about.

In a way this is how it was for Jesus. He left behind his divine beauty and strength to take on a human body and soul with all its limitations. He had to teach us about the Kingdom of Heaven, in a way we could understand.

Think about those snails again. They have never seen an airplane or tasted a chocolate chip cookie. Chances are they would not believe what you told them about these things.

They think the snail world is the only world. Besides, you are a snail just like them. Who do you think you are, claiming to be a human coming from this world of man?

You can see that you would have to care about those snails a great deal if you were to stay and keep trying to teach them. Jesus loved us a great deal. That is why he came to live with us.

There is more. Because God has honored the human race by becoming one of us, we now have a greatness we did not have before. Our eyes, ears, hands, feet, and souls are greater gifts of God than ever before, now that he has had them too. Our sorrows and our joys have more dignity because Jesus experienced human joys and sorrows as well. Everyday things, such as the cry of a baby, a game of tag, or a family dinner, have special meaning because the Son of God has shared them. Because God has become closer to us, we are now closer to God.

***

In obedience to Jewish law, Mary and Joseph took the Infant Jesus to the Temple to present him to the Lord. This was the rule for all firstborn sons. There an old man named Simeon was filled with joy. God had once promised that he would see the Savior before he died. The Holy Spirit let Simeon know that the baby carried by Mary and Joseph was that Savior.

He took the child in his arms and praised God. Simeon predicted that Jesus would bring God's grace to all men, not only the Jews, when he called Jesus ''a light to reveal you to the Gentiles.''—he also warned Mary that one day, she would suffer with Jesus: ''Your own heart shall be pierced by a sword.''

Jesus was to have enemies very early in his earthly life. When the Magi arrived in Jerusalem asking directions to the house of the ''newborn king of the Jews'', King Herod was enraged. *Nobody* was to take his place as king of the Jews, whatever the prophecies said! His only thought was to destroy this new king. Herod tried to trick the Magi into helping him, but an angel warned the Magi not to trust Herod. Then this evil ruler ordered that all baby boys in Bethlehem were to be killed.

By the time the order was carried out the Holy Family was well on its way to safety in Egypt because an angel had warned Joseph in a dream. They stayed there until Herod died and God told them they could return to Nazareth. Jesus grew up like any other boy of his time. Everyone thought Joseph was Jesus' real father; they did not know that he was just his foster (putative) father. No one but Mary and Joseph knew that God-made-man walked among them.

Words to Know:

Incarnation   nativity

The Word of God, Jesus Christ, on account of his great love for mankind, became what we are in order to make us what he is himself.

— St. Irenaeus

"I believe . . . in Jesus Christ . . . who was conceived of the Holy Spirit, born of the Virgin Mary. . . ."

Q. 45 *How was the Son of God made man?*
The Son of God was made man by taking a body and a soul, like we have, in the pure womb of the Virgin Mary, by the work of the Holy Spirit.

Q. 46 *Did the Son of God cease being God when he was made man?*
When the Son of God was made man he did not cease being God but, remaining true God, began to be also true man.

Q. 47 *Are there two natures in Jesus Christ?*
In Jesus Christ there are two natures: the divine nature and the human nature.

Q. 48 *With the two natures in Jesus Christ are there also two persons?*
With the two natures in Jesus Christ there are not two persons but only one, the divine person of the Son of God.

Q. 49 *Did Jesus Christ always exist?*
As God, Jesus Christ has always existed; as man, he began to exist from the moment of the Incarnation.

Q. 50 *From whom was Jesus Christ born?*
Jesus Christ was born of Mary ever-virgin, who therefore is called and truly is the Mother of God.

Q. 51 *But was not Saint Joseph the father of Jesus Christ?*
Saint Joseph was not the *true* father of Jesus Christ, but the *putative* father; that is, as the spouse of Mary and the guardian of Jesus, he was *believed* to be his true father, although actually he was not.

Q. 52 *Where was Jesus Christ born?*
Jesus Christ was born at Bethlehem, in a stable, and was placed in a manger.

CHAPTER 13

The Holy Family

The time between the Holy Family's return from Egypt and the baptism of Jesus we call the "hidden years" or the "private life" of Our Lord. Except for the time the Holy Family travelled to Jerusalem when Jesus was twelve, the Gospels tell us nothing about these years.

Because of this, we can guess that Jesus lived a very ordinary life with his parents. The time had not yet come for him to begin his public ministry. So he did not work any miracles or preach any sermons. To the people of Nazareth Jesus was just another boy. The scriptures say that Christ was like us in all things but sin.

Much of the same can be said for Our Lady and Saint Joseph. Both of them led lives of extraordinary holiness and goodness. Yet there was nothing unusual about their daily routines. Joseph earned a living as a carpenter, making tables and benches in his workshop, and perhaps helping people to build their homes. Without the drills and power saws of today, carpentry was hard work. Joseph must have been tired at the day's end.

As for Mary, she did not need to look for an outside job to keep busy. Her job was to use Joseph's earnings wisely for the care of their family. She probably had to go to the market each day for food. She very likely made all the clothes and perhaps even wove the cloth. Since homes had no running water in those days,

Mary must have had to carry jars of water from the town well. In addition, Mary must have done what she could to help others like visiting the sick and giving to those who were very poor and hungry.

You can be sure that Jesus helped Joseph and Mary with their many tasks. And we know that the Holy Family's life was not one of unending work. They set aside time to relax and enjoy one another. They spent time in family prayer. The Sabbath was a special day of worship.

As mentioned earlier, Jesus went to Jerusalem with his parents when he was twelve years old. It was the time of Passover, the holiest feast of the Jews. When Mary and Joseph started back for Nazareth, they did not know that Jesus stayed behind. They thought he was with some of their many friends and relatives who were also making the trip. A day had passed before Mary and Joseph discovered their mistake. After three days of worried searching, they found Jesus in the Temple, talking about God with the priests and teachers. "All who heard him were amazed at his intelligence and his answers" (Lk 2:47).

Mary and Joseph did not understand why Jesus had caused them such sorrow. But perhaps Mary thought of Simeon's prophecy: "A sword will pierce your heart" (Lk 2:35). Being Mother of the Messiah took great faith, courage, and a readiness to accept suffering without always understanding why.

Jesus went back to Nazareth and was obedient to his parents. As God, he didn't have to obey anyone. But because he wanted to share our human life in every way, Jesus chose to respect the command God has given to children everywhere: "Honor your father and mother."

The Holy Family and You

The Holy Family teaches us some important lessons about ourselves and our role in our own families.

1. *Accept God's will for you*. Mary and Joseph did not expect God to "pay them back" for being good with riches and an easy life. Instead, they trusted God to do what was best for them. At God's command, Joseph "dropped everything" and moved his family to Egypt, then back again. We should all be ready to do what God wants, without question.

2. *Do the job you are meant to do in your family*. Parents and children are happiest when they work together for the good of the family. Think of a baseball game. If all the players crowded onto the pitcher's mound or if the pitcher tried to play second base the team would never win. Your job in your "family team" is to obey your parents and do your share. This was the job Jesus had. Obedience is not easy. But believe it or not, obedience prepares us for the days when we will no longer have to obey our parents as we do while we are children. By obediently listening to our parents, we will learn to do the things that we will need to do when we are living on our own.

3. *Make God a member of your family*. The family whose lives are centered on God is a happy family. Is there a crucifix, statue, or picture of Jesus (and one of Mary) in the part of the house where you spend the most time together? Does your family pray before meals? If you already do this, your family may wish to try more family prayer, such as the rosary or a daily Bible reading. Tell your parents what you learn in your religion lessons.

Talk with your parents about how your family can make Sunday a special family day. Perhaps you can all attend Mass together, have a special Sunday breakfast, and spend Sunday afternoon doing something you all enjoy.

4. *Do good for others as a family*. Many families find a way to help someone in need. Some put aside extra money each month for the missions. Others collect clothing for the poor in their community. Your family may have a special talent to share with others. One family that all like to sing joined the church choir. Another family that all like sports help out at the "Special Olympics".

Q. 53 *Why did Jesus Christ wish to be poor?*
Jesus Christ wished to be poor in order to teach us to be humble and not to place our happiness in the riches, the honors, and the pleasures of this world.

CHAPTER 14

The Kingdom of Heaven

When Jesus was thirty years old, the time had come for him to begin his mission. First, he went to see his cousin, John the Baptist. John was now a great prophet. Crowds of people came to hear him preach repentance and to be baptized as a sign of sorrow for their sins. Some people thought John was the Messiah, but John made it clear that he was only the Savior's herald: ''I am the voice of one crying in the wilderness . . . 'prepare the way of the Lord'. . . . One is coming who is greater than I, whose sandal I am not worthy to untie.''

So naturally, John was startled to see Jesus wading into the Jordan River. ''It is I who ought to be baptized by you'', he said. Jesus insisted, even though he did not need to be baptized. He wanted to share everything with the people, including their sorrow for sin. After Jesus was baptized the Holy Spirit came down upon him, and the voice of God the Father was heard to say: ''This is my beloved Son in whom I am well pleased.''

Jesus then went into the desert mountains to pray and to fast for forty days. He knew his work would be difficult, and he needed this time to prepare himself for it. At the end of the forty days, Satan came to tempt Jesus. He tried to persuade Jesus to make life easy for himself with his miraculous powers, to be a mighty earthly ruler, accepted by all. But Jesus wanted only the will of his Father. He would not and could not sin. He sent Satan away.

After coming back from the desert, Our Lord began preaching in the villages of Galilee. He spoke in synagogues, on the streets, by the lake shores, and on the hillsides. Jesus did not spend much time with the educated Pharisees

"The Kingdom of Heaven is like treasure hidden in a field, which a man found and covered up; then in his joy he goes and sells all that he has and buys that field."
(Matthew 13:44)

or the religious leaders of his day. He wanted to bring the Good News of salvation to the poor, to sinners, and to all whom the world considered unimportant. Among his disciples were simple fishermen and even a tax collector whom everyone had hated. The boys and girls of Galilee loved to be near Jesus. Here was a rabbi (religious teacher) who was a real friend to them!

Jesus taught the people truths about God, about Heaven, and about the way to get to Heaven. He said that God loved them like a Father and was longing for sinners to come back to him. Jesus spoke of the Kingdom of Heaven, whose members would be not merely servants, but children of God. Children of the Kingdom were to have a way of life that would reflect God's love. They were to love all men, even their enemies. They were to forgive and pray for those who sinned against them. Jesus said they would be judged by how they treated the hungry, the sick, the imprisoned, and all who could not help themselves.

To help people understand better what the Kingdom of Heaven was, Jesus told short stories called parables. "The Kingdom of

> The Kingdom of God is the Kingdom of love. Those who love possess his Kingdom within them; those who lack love do not belong to it, and God reigns not in them.
>
> — St. Augustine

Heaven is like a mustard seed", said Jesus in one of his parables. "It is the smallest of seeds. But when it grows, it is greater than other plants. It becomes a tree" (Mt 13:31—32). This helps us see that the work of Christ and his Church began in a small, hidden way. It seemed unimportant to the world, like the mustard seed. But the Kingdom would grow until it became the greatest spiritual kingdom in the world. Like the mustard tree, it would tower over the kingdoms of men.

At another time, Jesus said the Kingdom of Heaven was like a giant fishnet let down into the water. "And when it was full the men pulled it out and, sitting by the shore, they gathered the good fish into containers and the bad they threw away" (Mt 13:47—51). At the end of the world, God will gather all men together and separate the good from the bad. In the meantime, it is not our job to judge each other, just as the fish could not decide by themselves who was good and who was bad. Judging fish is the job of the fisherman; judging souls is best left to God.

One of the most beautiful parables is about a treasure in a field (Mt 13:44). A man was digging in the ground when he discovered a buried treasure. Knowing the value of the treasure, he sold all that he owned, and with that money bought the land where the treasure was hidden. When we discover the Kingdom of Heaven, we have found the greatest treasure of all. We do not mind giving our lives to Jesus, because in exchange he will give us eternal life in Heaven. Other people may not understand why we follow Christ. Perhaps the man in the parable looked stupid to others, giving his life savings for a plot of worthless land. They did not know about the hidden treasure. In the same way, the joys of Heaven are hidden from many people today. But those who have found the Kingdom of Heaven know it is worth any price

***

Jesus chose twelve men to be his closest friends, his apostles. They were to spend more time with Jesus than anyone else. Someday they would carry on his work by preaching, baptizing, and leading the Church he founded.

In all things, Jesus chose to do the will of his Father. The long miles from town to town tired him. The refusal of some to listen to the Good News saddened him. But through it all, Jesus was happy knowing that he was carrying out his Father's plan to save the world and conquer sin. "I have come to do the will of him who sent me", said Jesus, even though the Father's will would one day lead him to pain and death. Jesus knew this, but he went ahead bravely, out of love for his Father and love for us.

Words to Know:

parable

means short stories

O Jesus, Master, establish your Kingdom in us: "a Kingdom of truth and life, of holiness and grace, a Kingdom of justice, love, and peace."

(Preface, Mass of Christ the King)

59

"This is my beloved Son, with whom I am well pleased; listen to him."   *(Matthew 17:5)*

CHAPTER 15

The Father and I Are One

In the last chapter, we learned that Christ taught people about the Heavenly Father who loved them and offered them the way to eternal life. But there was another part of Christ's teaching. It was so unusual, and so surprising, that Jesus did not even tell people about it at first. He only gave hints of it now and then. And sometimes, when people found out, Jesus would tell them not to tell anyone else.

What was this mysterious news that Jesus only let out little by little? It was the truth that Jesus Christ was the Son of God, both human and divine. The Jews were not at all ready for this truth. They thought the Messiah would be a man, a descendant of David who would restore the kingdom of Israel. They also thought the Messiah would be a holy leader who would show them how to become closer to God. But God's Son? The idea of a man claiming to be God sounded like *blasphemy*, a sin against the Second Commandment. So you can see why Jesus had to be patient and careful about telling the people who he really is.

The first hints Jesus gave of his divinity were his miracles. With a word or a touch, he healed people of blindness, leprosy, and many other diseases. On two occasions he multiplied bread to feed thousands of people. Since no prophet had ever done these things, people could see that Jesus shared God's power in a special way. Jesus could also heal people who

were possessed by devils. (When someone is "possessed" the devil controls his speech and actions so completely that the person has no power to stop it.) The Gospels tell us that these devils knew who Jesus was, but that Jesus ordered them to keep silent. The time had not yet come for a clear statement of Christ's divinity, and the devil was not the right one to make such a statement.

Jesus allowed his apostles to learn the truth sooner. They saw him stop a storm with a single command, and they wondered, "Who is this, that even the wind and sea obey him?" (Lk 8:24−25). At another time, the apostles were again caught in a storm on the lake, but Jesus was not with them. Late at night, they were astonished to see Jesus walking across the water toward them. Peter asked if he might come to Jesus across the water, so Jesus said, "Come." Peter was able to walk on the water until he grew afraid; then he sank. Jesus pulled Peter back up and took him to the boat. The other apostles, says the Gospel, "worshipped him and said, 'Truly you are the Son of God'" (Mt 14:33).

Later, Jesus asked the apostles, "Who do men say that I am?" They reported what people were saying: that Jesus was Elijah or one of the prophets come back to earth; perhaps John the Baptist. Then Jesus asked, "But who do *you* say that I am?" Peter replied, "You are the

Christ, the Son of the Living God." Jesus told Peter he was correct: "Flesh and blood has not revealed this to you, but my Father in Heaven." But still Jesus told the apostles not to tell anyone else that he was God's Son (Mt 16:13—20).

Even with this new knowledge of Jesus' true identity, it must have been hard for the apostles to understand. After all, Jesus looked so ordinary. When God visited his people in the Scriptures, there were always signs of his glory and power such as fiery clouds, thunder, or brilliant light. Jesus had kept his glory hidden, but one day, he revealed it to Peter, James, and John. He took them up a mountain,

> and was transfigured before them. His face shone as the sun, and his garments became white as snow. And behold, there appeared Moses and Elijah talking together with him. . . . A bright cloud overshadowed them, and a voice came out of the cloud saying "This is my beloved Son, in whom I am well pleased; hear him." (Mt 17:1—5)

When the vision ended, Jesus again looked as he always did. He told the three apostles to tell no one what had happened until after the Resurrection.

The time finally came for Jesus to proclaim his divinity to the people more openly. Once, in the Temple of Jerusalem, Jesus said, "Before Abraham was, I am." Many were horrified and picked up stones to throw at Jesus. Not only did he claim to have lived before Abraham, but he took as his own the sacred Name of God, "I AM", that had been revealed to Moses. Those who hated Jesus considered this a crime. They plotted to kill him.

The poor and simple people of Jerusalem were more ready to believe. Jesus cured a blind man and later asked him, "Do you believe in the Son of God?" "Who is he, Lord," replied the man, "that I may believe in him?" "You have seen him", said Jesus. "It is he who now speaks to you." And the man fell to his knees to worship Jesus (Jn 9:35—38).

Jesus showed his divine power again when he raised Lazarus from the dead. "I am the Resurrection and the life", said Jesus. The people knew that God would not give such wonderful powers to Jesus if he was telling a lie about being God's Son.

The greatest proof of Jesus' divinity would be his Resurrection from the dead. But that was yet to come.

Words to Know:

blasphemy   divinity   transfiguration

Q. 54 *How was Jesus Christ known to be the Son of God?*
Jesus Christ was known to be the Son of God because God the Father proclaimed him as such at his baptism and his transfiguration, when he said: "This is my beloved Son, in whom I am well pleased." And also because Jesus Christ himself declared himself to be the Son of God during his earthly life (Mt 3:17; Lk 9:35).

Q. 55 *What is a miracle?*

A miracle is something beyond all the forces and laws of nature, and therefore something which can be worked only by God, who is the Lord and Master of nature.

Q. 56 *With what miracles in particular did Jesus Christ confirm his doctrine and demonstrate that he is true God?*

Jesus Christ confirmed his teaching and demonstrated that he is true God by instantly restoring vision to the blind, hearing to the deaf, speech to the dumb, health to sick persons of every type, and life to the dead. And also, as their Lord and Master by commanding the demons and the forces of nature. Above all, he did so with his own Resurrection from the dead.

CHAPTER 16

Your Sins Are Forgiven

Our Lord gradually revealed himself to his apostles and others as the Son of God. He made his divinity known by performing miracles. Jesus showed his authority over sickness, devils, the wind and sea, even death itself. There was something else Jesus did that told people that Jesus was God, even when he did not say it in so many words: Jesus *forgave sins*.

"What is so special about that?" you might ask. Imagine that a friend told you that he had cheated on a test or stolen money from his mother's purse. If you then said, "I forgive you", your friend would think you were crazy. What right would you have to forgive when *you* were not the one who was hurt by the sin?

Yet this was exactly what Jesus did. When a paralyzed man was brought to him, Jesus said, "Your sins are forgiven." This would make sense only if Jesus were God, because every sin, whoever it may hurt on earth, also breaks God's laws and wounds his love. Some of the Pharisees who were watching Jesus were angry and upset at his words. "Who is this man to speak blasphemies? Who but God can forgive sins?", they thought to themselves.

Jesus knew their thoughts, and he decided to prove that he had the power to forgive sins. When the people brought him a paralyzed man, he asked, "Which is easier, to say to the paralytic, 'Your sins are forgiven', or to say, 'Stand up, pick up your mat, and walk again'?

That you may know that the Son of Man has the authority on earth to forgive sins [he said to the paralyzed man], 'I command you: Stand up! Pick up your mat, and go home' " (Mk 2:9−11).

And with that, the man could walk. Jesus was right. Anybody could claim to forgive sins—no one could "see" sins being forgiven. But to heal a man who had not walked in years—everyone could see that. The people realized that Jesus meant what he said, that he really could forgive sins.

As glad as Jesus was to heal people of pain and sickness, he really came to heal their souls from sin. Many people in Jesus' time believed that they were too sinful to be forgiven. The Pharisees had taught them that one could not please God unless he observed Jewish law without a single mistake. Jesus, on the other hand, tried to convince the people that God was always ready to forgive. All the person had to do was repent of his sin and ask God's forgiveness. Jesus taught that God was happier over one sinner who repents than any number of good people who do not need to repent. To illustrate this truth he told the parable of the lost sheep and the parable of the prodigal son. You can read these parables in Luke 15.

Inspired by this new message of God's compassion, sinners came to Jesus, seeking forgiveness. When Jesus forgave them, they often found the power to become saints. Mary Magdalen turned from a life of impurity to become one of Jesus' most faithful followers. Zacchaeus, a tax collector who was seen as a traitor by the Jews, promised to give half of his money to the poor and return four times the amount of any money he had taken from others. The good thief who died on the cross next to Jesus received the gift of eternal life, ''This day you will be with me in Paradise.''

Jesus asked us to imitate God's readiness to forgive. We should gladly forgive others who sin against us, no matter how often it happens. We must forgive others if we want to be forgiven ourselves. Every day we pray in the Lord's prayer, ''Forgive us our trespasses as we forgive those who trespass against us.'' With these words we are asking God to forgive us *as much* as we forgive others. We should think hard about this, especially if we are in the habit of staying angry for a long time at those who hurt us. We certainly would not want God to behave this way toward us. So we must act quickly to forgive anyone who wrongs us.

How do you forgive someone? There are different ways to forgive. For example, if a brother or sister comes to you saying, ''I am sorry for what I did'', your job is to say, ''I forgive you'' or, ''That's okay'' and then *show that you mean it*. Act as if nothing had happened. Be extra friendly for a while, to make the ''sinner'' feel better.

What if the ''sinner'' does not want to be forgiven? Perhaps there is someone who has decided not to like you and who tries to say and do things that hurt you whenever he can? Such a person might only laugh if you said, ''I forgive you''. Sometimes people hurt us because they think we do not like them. You might say to this person, ''Let's be friends'', or ask him to join you and your friends in a game. But if an offer of friendship will not work, then simply forgive the sinner in your heart. And pray for him every day. Prayer can do much to change other people.

Words to Know:

forgiveness

''If we confess our sins, he is faithful and just, and will forgive our sins and cleanse us from all unrighteousness.''
(1 John 1:9)

CHAPTER 17

True God and True Man

After talking so much about Christ's divinity, we must spend some time on his humanity as well. Although the Jews found it hard to believe that Jesus was God, today we sometimes find it hard to realize that Jesus is truly man. Some of the statues and pictures of Jesus that we see can give Jesus a stiff, unreal look. We sometimes think that Jesus was not really a man but, rather, God "disguised" as a man. This is not true at all. If it were, Jesus would never have felt hunger, thirst, or the need for sleep. But in fact he felt all of these things. The Gospels give us many glimpses of a Savior who was fully human: getting tired of having too many people around at times, falling asleep in a boat while the apostles battled a storm, enjoying the company of little children, building a campfire and fixing breakfast for his apostles. Jesus took part in everything our human life has to offer. As the Epistle to the Hebrews states, he was "like us in all things but sin".

As God the Son, Jesus existed from all eternity. At a certain point in history, he took on a human nature and was born of the Virgin Mary. (A human nature includes not only a body but a human mind and soul as well.) From then on, Jesus had two natures, divine and human. Yet, he remained one Person, not two. You will remember from Chapter 2 that "nature" means "what you are" and "person"

means "who you are". If you asked Jesus, "What are you?", he would say "God and man". We do not know exactly how the union of the divine and human natures "works". It is one of the mysteries of our faith which we will not fully understand even in Heaven, though we will understand it much better there.

In his love, the Father sent Jesus to be an example for us. It is one thing to hear sermon after sermon about obeying God's law. But Jesus taught us how to obey the Father by the way he lived. He showed real love to everyone. He forgave his enemies. Most important, he obeyed his Father in everything. Obedience is hard for all of us. It may mean setting aside our own plans and wishes to carry out those of someone else. It may mean doing things we do not like, doing them because God has told us to.

But God's own Son showed us that he, too, would humbly obey God's plan for him. As man, Jesus did not like the idea of pain and death any more than the rest of us. But he wanted to do the will of his Father whom he loved, so he went to his death freely and bravely. When we remember that even God's Son, the Lord of the Universe, was willing to obey, it should help us to obey as well.

Jesus became man in order to be, not just our Savior, but also our brother and friend. We can talk to him about our joys, our problems, and our temptations. He will always understand. If ever we are not sure what to do, we can ask in prayer, ``Jesus, what would you do if this happened to you?'' Then he will remind us of what is right and wrong, and he will give us the courage to do what is right. If we should fall into sin, we can turn to Jesus, knowing he wants to forgive us and restore us to his friendship.

Christ as God is the fatherland where
    we are going;
Christ as Man is the way by which we go.

— St. Augustine

CHAPTER 18

Rejected by the Proud

Many a person has thought, "If only I had lived in Palestine in the days of Jesus. It would be so easy to believe in him, after seeing his miracles with my own eyes. And it would be easy to love God and be holy after getting to meet Jesus and talking to him."

Would it really be easier? If so, then what was wrong with all the people who saw the miracles, heard Jesus teach, yet did not believe? Yes, if you, a Christian who had received the gift of faith at Baptism, could have gone back in time to meet Jesus, it probably would have increased your faith. But if you had been a first-century Jew, it might have been a different story.

As we saw before, the Jewish people lived in expectation of the coming Messiah. Even among themselves, however, they did not agree on what he would do when he came. The Jews were divided into groups: Pharisees, Sadducees, scribes, Essenes, Zealots, Herodians. (The names of some of these you may recognize from the Gospel stories you have heard or read.) Each group had its own idea of what the Messiah should be; each group thought he should be one of them. It turned out that Jesus did not fit the pattern of any of them.

Instead of spending his time with scribes, Pharisees, and other important people, Jesus more often gave his attention to the ordinary people, fishermen, farmers, housewives. He told stories to children. He even took his meals with people known to be great sinners. To the important people, this did not seem to be proper behavior for the Messiah.

The people were so certain that the promised Savior would look and act a certain way that, when Jesus was different, they did not accept him. Even though there were miracles, it still took faith to believe that God sent a different kind of Savior.

Many of the people who liked Jesus turned away on the day he first mentioned the Holy Eucharist. "I am the living bread . . . the bread I will give is my Flesh for the life of the world" (Jn 6:51). To most of the people the idea of eating another man's flesh sounded strange and sinful. Many did not have enough faith to stay with Jesus and wait for the time when the mystery of the Eucharist would be made more clear to them.

The Jewish leaders were not merely upset about Jesus. They actually hated him. For the Pharisees, Jesus did not seem to have proper respect for the Law of Moses. For the Sadducees, Jesus seemed to be stirring up unrest among the people. The scribes were probably disturbed because Jesus did not consult them on the interpretation of the Law. Jesus did not identify himself with any of the leaders or with the groups. It is quite the opposite. He was bold enough to tell them where they were

wrong, saying of the Pharisees, for example, that they were ''hypocrites'' and comparing them to whitewashed tombs, beautiful on the outside but decayed and ugly on the inside.

It was common Jewish thought that great wealth was a sign of God's favor, and poverty a punishment from God on those who sinned. On the contrary, said Jesus, ''It is easier for a camel to pass through the eye of a needle than for a rich man to enter the Kingdom of Heaven.'' Jesus taught that God had a special love for the poor and suffering.

What made these religious leaders resent Jesus most of all was his popularity. The people loved to listen to him, and follow the way of life Jesus preached. The Pharisees, scribes, and priests became jealous. They tried again and again to get Jesus to say something that was against God's law. They would ask Jesus difficult questions, not in order to learn, but in the hope of catching him in some mistake. But Jesus always found a way to make the truth clear, and show the falsehood of his questioners.

The enemies of Jesus witnessed many of his miracles. But they did not *want* Jesus to be the Messiah. Believing in him would force them to repent of their sins and change their lives in too many ways. They were too proud to admit that the man they hated might be God's Son. So they told themselves that all those wonderful miracles were the work of the devil. They wanted to kill Jesus and set to work planning to do so.

Turning away from Jesus

Jesus was rejected by many of the religious leaders and people of his time, but this rejection was not a one-time event. Every time someone commits a mortal sin he turns away from Jesus. To commit a mortal sin is to act as if Jesus does not belong in one's life.

Even when we commit only a venial sin, we show that we do not love Jesus as much as we ought to. We are like the apostles, who loved Our Lord but ran away when things became difficult.

If we look around us we can see that in many ways our society rejects Jesus. We hear many use his Holy Name in a careless or angry way. The characters in many TV shows and movies act as if Jesus did not exist. All around us we see that God's gift of human life is not treated with love and reverence.

Since Jesus is rejected in so many ways by so many, we want to do what we can to make up for this. By refusing to go along with a godless world, we accept and honor Jesus and show ourselves to be his true friends.

''Jesus said to the Twelve, 'Will you also go away?'

''Simon Peter answered him, 'Lord, to whom shall we go? You have the words of eternal life; and we have believed, and have come to know, that you are the Holy One of God.' ''

(John 6:67—69)

CHAPTER 19

The Acceptance of The Father's Will

As the time for Passover drew near, Jesus came to Jerusalem. At this time of year, thousands of Jews were visiting the holy city. Word had spread that Jesus was coming. The people gathered in great excitement. They had heard how Jesus brought Lazarus back to life only a few days before. As Jesus rode into the city, the crowd shouted joyfully, ''Blessed is he who comes in the name of the Lord, the King of Israel!'' They waved palm branches and laid them down on the road before Jesus. They even placed their coats on the dusty ground in order to make a welcoming carpet for him to pass over. The priests and Pharisees watched in anger. The people no longer cared what these men had to say against Jesus. ''Look! The entire world has run after him'', they muttered. They decided to speed up their plans to put Jesus to death.

As for Jesus, he knew that the excitement of the crowd would die down in a few days time. He knew that most of these people would not be around to protest his death sentence or comfort him as he suffered. Several times in the past months, Jesus warned his disciples of what would happen. ''The Son of Man will be delivered to the Gentiles, and he will be mocked and scourged and spit upon. . . . They will put him to death, and on the third day he will rise again'' (Lk 18:31−33). The Gospel tells us that the disciples did not understand when Jesus spoke to them like this. The words were clear enough, but perhaps the disciples found the idea of Jesus' death just too terrible to accept. Like most people, the disciples were expecting Jesus to use his powers to set himself up as king of Israel. They still did not see that Jesus came to earth to save us from our sins and lead us to a heavenly Kingdom.

But Jesus clearly understood what his Father wanted of him. He accepted the Cross, knowing that his act of obedience would save the world from sin and death. He mentioned it

The children of Jerusalem welcomed Christ the King. They carried olive branches and loudly praised the Lord: Hosanna in the highest.

(Palm Sunday Procession Antiphon)

several times while preaching to the people. In the parable of the Good Shepherd, Jesus pointed out that he was not going to be trapped into death against his will but that he would choose it freely: "I lay down my life for my sheep. No one *takes* it from me; I lay it down freely, and I have the power to take it up again" (Jn 10:18). Another time Jesus made it plain that he had to die for the good of others, "Unless a grain of wheat falls into the ground and dies, it remains by itself. But if it dies, it brings forth much fruit" (Jn 12:24−25).

The Last Supper

Knowing the end was near, Jesus gathered his disciples for their last Passover supper together. The disciples had been quarreling over which of them most deserved to sit close to Jesus when he established his Kingdom. Without a word, Jesus taught them a great lesson in humility. He took the place of a servant and washed their feet.

The disciples were astonished and saddened when Jesus said that one of them would betray him. He identified Judas, who then got up and left. Most of the disciples, however, did not realize what was happening and thought that Jesus had sent Judas on an errand.

There came a moment at the Last Supper that was important not only for the disciples, but for every Christian who would ever live. Our Lord took bread, blessed it, broke it, and said, "Take this. . . . This is my Body." Then he took a cup of wine: "This is my Blood, which will be shed for you and for many, for the forgiveness of sins." This was the first Holy Eucharist. We say that Holy Thursday is the day Christ *instituted* (began) the Holy Eucharist. On this day, he also gave the disciples the power to consecrate the bread and wine. "Do this in memory of me." The Last Supper was the very first Mass.

***

After the Last Supper, Jesus took his disciples to the Garden of Gethsemane. There he began to feel afraid at the very thought of the sufferings he would undergo. "Father," Jesus prayed, "if it is possible, take this cup away from me. Yet, not as I will, but as you will."

The thought of our sins and ingratitude hurt the loving Heart of Jesus even more than the thought of dying. In his sorrow and agony, Jesus began to sweat blood. God the Father sent an angel to comfort Jesus and strengthen him for the terrible hours ahead.

Judas came, leading a crowd of Temple guards and soldiers to arrest Jesus. The disciples ran away, and Jesus was taken before Caiaphas, the high priest. The chief priest accused him of blasphemy, and he and the other members of the Sanhedrin (the Jewish leaders) sentenced him to death. But being under the rule of the Roman government, they could not carry out this sentence legally. So they took Jesus before Pontius Pilate, the Roman governor of Judea. The Jewish leaders attempted to convince Pilate that Jesus was a dangerous criminal who wanted to overthrow the Roman emperor. Pilate knew there was no case against Jesus, and he tried to satisfy the angry crowd by having Jesus scourged. But

". . . suffered under Pontius Pilate, was crucified, died, and was buried. . . ."

the crowd insisted that Jesus be put to death. Pilate, afraid of the people, finally agreed to have Jesus crucified.

Scripture and tradition tell us of the painful journey Jesus made, carrying the Cross to Calvary. Only one of the disciples, John, along with Mary and a few of Jesus' women followers, were with him as he hung upon the Cross. Before he died, Jesus asked the Father to forgive his enemies. Even in his most painful moments, he thought of others with love: he forgave the good thief and promised, "This day you will be with me in Paradise." He saw his mother with his youngest disciple, and said, "Woman, behold your son. Son, behold your Mother." With these words, Jesus gave Mary to the whole world, to be spiritual Mother to all God's children.

Our Lord's last words were a final act of surrender to the will of the Father. "Father, into your hands I commend my spirit." With these words, Jesus died.

Q. 57 *What did Jesus Christ accomplish during his earthly life?*

During his earthly life Jesus Christ taught us by his example and his word to live according to God, and he confirmed his doctrine by his miracles. Finally, to cancel our debt of sin, to reconcile us with God, and to reopen Heaven to us, he sacrificed himself on the Cross, "the only mediator between God and men" (1 Tim 2:5).

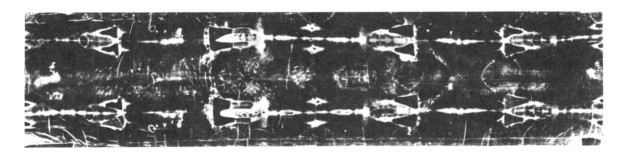

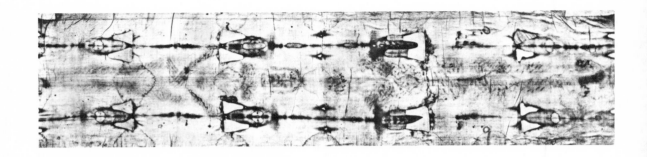

The Shroud of Turin

The Shroud of Turin is one of the most treasured possessions of the Church. It is believed to be the burial cloth of Jesus. On the shroud is an imprint of the crucified Christ. The image is very detailed, which especially shows when it is photographed and turned into a negative. We can see the marks of the nails in the hands and feet of Our Lord, the wounds from the scourging and crown of thorns, and the wound in his side from the soldier's spear.

In recent years, scientists of all faiths have been studying the Shroud of Turin. They have made many discoveries that support the belief that the Shroud is truly the burial cloth of Jesus, and that the image on it is miraculous.

CHAPTER 20

The Perfect Sacrifice

To sacrifice is to give up something we would rather keep, for the love of God or neighbor. There are many ways to sacrifice. You may give up some of your money to help the poor or give up some of your free time to help your mother when she is tired. The value of a sacrifice does not always depend on the size of the thing one gives up. Once Jesus watched some people offering money in the Temple. Some people gave large amounts, but since they were very rich their sacrifices were not great. Then, a poor widow came, and she offered two copper coins of little value. Jesus remarked that her sacrifice was worth more than all the others' because it was all she had to live on.

Mankind has had a long tradition of offering sacrifices to God in response to God's command and as a way to show sorrow for sin, to show love for God, and to thank God for the good things he has given them. At the very beginning of the Bible, Cain and Abel, the sons of Adam and Eve, made sacrifices of their crops and animals to the Lord.

The Jewish people made the offering of sacrifice a regular part of their worship. They would bring to the Temple the best of what their farms produced. If it were an animal, such as a lamb, calf, or goat, the priests would slaughter it and sprinkle its blood upon the altar. Offerings of wine were poured over the altar, and cakes of fine wheat flour were burned. When Mary and Joseph presented the infant Jesus in the Temple, they brought along two doves as a sacrifice (Lk 2:24).

Although God was pleased with many of

these offerings and sacrifices, they were not enough to make up for sin and completely restore mankind to its original friendship with God. Without sanctifying grace, no one could make a perfect sacrifice. That is why Jesus came. As the sinless man, he could make the acceptable sacrifice. As the sinless man, he could make that sacrifice on behalf of the human race. In this supreme sacrifice, Jesus was both priest and victim. In other words, he not only took the place of the victim (the animal) that was offered to God by a priest, but he was himself the priest as well. The role of the priest was to stand between God and mankind to make the offering. Jesus, being both God and man, was the perfect "link" between Heaven and earth. He offered, not an animal, but himself, as the sacrifice for sin. In the Gospel, John the Baptist called Jesus the "Lamb of God". Just as the blood of a slaughtered lamb saved each Hebrew family from death in Egypt, the blood of Christ saves us from the eternal death that comes from sin.

Until Christ's saving sacrifice, Heaven had been closed to all who had died since the time of Adam. This did not mean that all souls were suffering in Hell. The souls of those who had lived good lives (Noah, Abraham, Saint Joseph, and many others) were in a place of waiting. (The Apostles' Creed calls this place *Hell*, although it was not the same as the Hell of eternal punishment.) When Jesus died, he released the souls of the just men and women who had died in the past. Finally they could live with God in Heaven. The sacrifice of Jesus was great enough to save all mankind: those from the past, those who lived at the time of the Incarnation, and all those who would ever live in the future.

Jesus opened Heaven and won back, or *redeemed*, the souls of all mankind. Now the gift of sanctifying grace would be available to all in the sacrament of Baptism.

> *Sing, my tongue, the Savior's glory;*
> *Tell his triumph far and wide;*
> *Tell aloud the famous story*
> *Of his body crucified;*
> *How upon the Cross a victim,*
> *Vanquishing in death, he died.*
>   *(Holy Thursday Hymn)*

The Sacrifice Goes on

Although Jesus died at one moment in history, the saving action of God is an eternal act. Jesus will not die again, but his saving grace will go out to all the earth until the end of time. To perpetuate his redemptive act, Our Lord instituted the Holy Sacrifice of the Mass. The Mass is a re-presentation of the same sacrifice Jesus made two thousand years ago. The priest takes the place of Christ, and he changes bread and wine into the Body and Blood of Our Savior. Remember, Jesus gave his apostles the power to do this at the Last Supper. Later, the apostles passed this power on to other men, and this has continued for centuries, right up to the priests we have today. So at the Mass, through the priest, Jesus offers himself to the Father.

When we participate in the Mass, we share in the priest's action by offering ourselves along with Jesus as a sacrifice to God. There is no better way to pray than to join ourselves to Jesus, in the Sacrifice of the Mass. Christ chooses ordinary bread and wine to make into his Body and Blood. When we give him our own ordinary, sinful souls, he can also make us into something wonderful: a precious gift to God.

Words to Know:

sacrifice

76

Persecutions

The Mass is the way in which Christ's saving grace goes out to the world. It is no wonder, then, that throughout history it has been under attack. But brave Christians were always willing to risk anything for the Holy Sacrifice.

In England during the late 1500s, the Protestant Queen Elizabeth I made it a crime to attend Mass. Priests had to travel in disguise from one Catholic home to another to celebrate Mass in secret. Catholic families built secret compartments in the walls or floors of their homes to hide the sacred vessels and other items needed to celebrate Mass. Sometimes, if government officials arrived, it was necessary for the visiting priest to squeeze into these hiding places. Many of these priests were caught and hanged, as were some of the lay people. Some of them are now saints of the Church, because they were martyrs.

In North America in the 1600s, Indians who became Christians had to face persecution if they participated in Mass. One of them, Blessed Kateri Tekawitha, was chased all the way to the church by the pagan Indians of her tribe. They threw stones at her and threatened her with tomahawks. Her own family would not let her eat on Sundays if she went to Mass. But Kateri loved God more than her own life, and she refused to give up going to Mass.

Even today, in Russia, communist police watch to see who goes to church on Sunday. Their names are taken down, and these people are usually not allowed good-paying jobs or nice houses. But the Mass means more to them than any earthly treasures.

Q. 58 *Did Jesus Christ die as God or as man?*
Jesus Christ died as man, because as God he could neither suffer nor die.

CHAPTER 21

He Is Risen

Early in the morning on the Sunday after Jesus died, Mary Magdalen and some other women walked along the road that led to the tomb. They wanted to complete the Jewish burial customs and annoint the body of Jesus with spices. There had not been enough time for this earlier because the Jewish sabbath had begun Friday evening and lasted all day Saturday. During the sabbath it was forbidden to handle a dead body.

Although it may have been a beautiful spring morning, the women's hearts were not light. The teacher they had loved and honored as the Messiah was dead. The disciples were still hidden indoors, heartbroken over Jesus' death and in fear for their lives. On top of everything else, the women worried that they

would not be able to perform this last act of love, the annointing of their dead master. The tomb was shut with a large stone which they themselves could not move. And it did not seem likely that the Roman guards, sent to the tomb to keep Jesus' disciples away, were going to help them. It must have seemed to the women that the forces of evil had won a terrible victory.

Arriving at the tomb, they were astonished to see the stone rolled away. An angel sat upon the stone and said, "Do not be afraid, for I know you seek Jesus, who was crucified. *He is not here, for he has risen* just as he said. Come and see the place where the Lord was laid. Then go quickly, tell his disciples that he has risen'' (Mt 28:5—7).

The women rushed back to the house where the disciples were staying. The disciples did not know what to think of their story, but Peter and John immediately left to see the tomb, running all the way. Mary Magdalen ran back with them. They looked into the tomb. The linen cloths that had covered the body of Jesus were neatly folded and set aside. John knew that grave robbers would not do such a thing. He recalled what Jesus had said about rising again. Yes! That was it! It had actually happened! At this moment, John became the first disciple to believe in the Resurrection. Peter and John ran back again to tell the others what they saw.

But Mary Magdalen remained behind. Tired and distressed by all that had happened, she could not think clearly. All she knew was that the body of Jesus was gone, perhaps stolen by wicked men. She began to cry. She heard a voice behind her: "Woman, why are you weeping? Are you looking for someone?" Her eyesight blurred by tears, Mary thought it was the cemetery gardener. But when the man spoke again, his voice was unmistakable. "Mary", he said. Mary looked again, and there stood Jesus! "Master!" she replied, almost speechless with joy. Jesus sent her to tell the disciples.

***

Jesus had won the greatest victory of all. He had defeated sin and conquered death, the punishment for sin. His Resurrection showed all his followers that Jesus was truly the Son of God, the King of Kings and Lord of Lords. It was a sign that God had accepted the sacrifice which Jesus made to redeem us.

After the Resurrection, the body of Jesus was changed, or *glorified*. Now he was no longer restricted by his body as the rest of us are. He could disappear and appear anywhere he wanted. He could pass through walls and locked doors. He no longer suffered any pain or discomfort, such as hunger or thirst. At the same time, Jesus still had a real body. He was not a ghost, and when he appeared to his disciples he proved this by eating food and allowing them to touch him.

The Resurrection of Jesus is one of the central truths of our faith. Saint Paul said, "If Christ has not been raised . . . your faith is in vain" (useless). Because Jesus came to life again, our souls, dead from sin, become alive in sanctifying grace through Baptism. Because Jesus is alive for ever, we too can hope to live for ever in Heaven.

"He descended into Hell; the third day he arose again from the dead. . . ."

Q. 59 *After his death, what did Jesus Christ do?*
After his death, Jesus Christ descended in his soul to the souls of the just who had died up to that time, to take them with him into Paradise. Then he rose again from the dead, taking up his body which had been buried.

Q. 60 *How long did the body of Jesus Christ remain buried?*
The body of Jesus Christ remained buried three days, although they were not full days: from Friday evening to the day that we now call Easter Sunday.

Rejoice, heavenly powers!
Sing, choirs of angels!
Exult, all creation around God's throne!
Jesus Christ, our King, is risen!
Sound the trumpet of salvation!

Rejoice, O earth, in shining splendor,
radiant in the brightness of your King!
Christ has conquered!

Glory fills you!
Darkness vanishes for ever!

Rejoice, O Mother Church! Exult in glory!
The risen Savior shines upon you!
Let this place resound with joy,
echoing the mighty song of all God's people!

(Exsultet)

The Easter Vigil Mass

If possible try to go to the Easter Vigil Mass. It is held late on Holy Saturday evening. Even more than the other Easter Masses, the Easter Vigil Mass teaches us how the death and Resurrection of Jesus brought us to new life.

At the Vigil:

You will see the blessing of the new paschal candle. This candle is decorated with symbols of Christ. Besides being used during the Easter season, during the year it will be lit at Baptisms and funerals.

You will see the blessing of new baptismal water. You may be able to take some holy water home with you.

Very often, adults or older children who convert to the Catholic faith are baptized at the Easter Vigil Mass. For them and for us this is a wonderful way to see how Baptism is our own sharing in the death and Resurrection of Jesus.

You will have an opportunity to renew your baptismal vows.

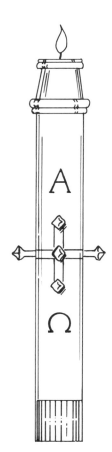

Christ yesterday and today,
the beginning and the end,
the alpha and the omega.

All time belongs to him
and all the ages:
to him be glory and power
through every age and for ever. *Amen.*

By his holy and glorious wounds
may Christ Our Lord guard us and keep us.
Amen.

(Prayer when the paschal candle is lit)

The Lord is risen from the grave, alleluia, alleluia, who hung for us upon the Tree, alleluia, alleluia.

CHAPTER 22

Jesus Sends the Apostles

During the days after the Resurrection on the first Easter Sunday, Jesus appeared to his friends many times. He used these visits to instruct them in the work of spreading the gospel and building up the Church on earth. He began this instruction the very first time he appeared to them. "As the Father has sent me, so I send you." Then he breathed on them and said, "Receive the Holy Spirit. If you forgive men's sins, they are forgiven them; if you hold them bound, they are held bound (Jn 20:21–23). And so Jesus gave the apostles a special power they would need as the first priests and bishops of the Church: the power to forgive sins. With this power, the apostles could bring God's mercy and forgiveness to all Christians. Later, they would pass this power on to others who would take their place.

One of the eleven apostles, Thomas, missed this meeting. He had not yet seen the risen Jesus and still did not believe. "Not until I see the nail marks in his hands, and put my hand into his side, will I believe such a thing", said Thomas. A week later, Jesus appeared again. This time Thomas was there. "Here Thomas, bring your finger and touch my hands", said Jesus. Put your hand into my side. Doubt no longer, but believe." "My Lord and my God", answered Thomas. (See Jn 20:24–29.)

We should find joy in the reply which Jesus made to Thomas because he mentioned us. He said, "Because you have seen, you believe. Blessed are they who do not see, yet believe all the same." We believe in Jesus although we have not seen him. Our faith will be rewarded.

Later, at the Sea of Tiberias the apostles decided to go fishing, just as they used to do before they had known Jesus. They spent the whole night on the lake, but caught nothing. As they rowed toward the shore the next morning, a man on the beach called out, "Did you catch anything?" When they told him, "No", he said, "Try throwing your net to the right of the boat. You will find something there." They followed the advice and pulled in a tremendous load of fish. "It is the Lord", shouted John. Peter remembered with joy the first time Jesus gave them a miraculous catch of fish. That had been the day he had called Peter to follow him. Now Peter quickly dived into the lake and swam to the beach while the other disciples brought in the boat and net full of fish. Jesus had built a fire, and he fixed them breakfast.

When they finished eating, Jesus stood up and spoke to Peter. He asked, "Do you love me?" Peter answered that he did, and Jesus replied, "Feed my lambs." Again Jesus asked whether Peter loved him. Peter answered, and Jesus said, "Feed my sheep." When Jesus asked a third time, "Do you love me?", Peter was upset. Did Jesus doubt him? "Please,

Lord, you know all things'', said Peter. ''You know I love you.'' Jesus again replied, ''Feed my sheep.''

With these words, Jesus again singled Peter out as the leader of his Church. He made Peter the shepherd of all—even of the other apostles. That is why Peter became leader of the Church on earth—the very first Pope.

After the forty days had passed, it was time for Jesus to return to his Father in Heaven. The disciples had learned much from Jesus during that time, but Jesus knew they needed something more before they could preach the gospel courageously and faithfully. He promised to send the Holy Spirit, who would give them the knowledge, faith, and power they needed.

Jesus led the Eleven, plus many of his other followers, up the slope of Mount Olivet. He gave his final instruction to the disciples:

> Full authority has been given to me both in Heaven and on earth; go, therefore, and make disciples of all the nations. Baptize them in the name of the Father, and of the Son, and of the Holy Spirit. Teach them to carry out everything I have commanded you. And know that I am with you always, until the end of the world. (Mt 28:18−20)

Then Jesus ascended into Heaven. ''He was lifted up before their eyes in a cloud which took him from their sight'' (Acts 1:10). As the apostles stared into the empty sky, two angels appeared. ''Men of Galilee, why do you stand here looking up at the sky? This Jesus who has been taken from you will return, just as you saw him go up into the Heavens'' (Acts 1:11).

"He ascended into Heaven and sits at the right hand of God the Father almighty. From thence he shall come to judge the living and the dead. . . ."

Recognizing Jesus in Others

The disciples did not recognize Jesus on the road to Emmaus. We, too, often have Jesus with us and do not even know it.

How can this be? Remember Our Lord's words in the Gospel: "Whenever you did it to the least of my brothers, you did it to me." Jesus is with us in the poor, the hungry, the sick, the lonely, and all those who need our love. When we think of helping the needy, we usually think of giving our money or donating food and clothing to people we will never see. But Jesus is present in everyone around us. The younger brother who is lonely and needs your friendship, the mother and father who need help with the chores around the house, the classmate whom no one likes: we should find Jesus in each one of them.

On a cold night many centuries ago, a soldier named Martin met a beggar who had on almost no clothes. Martin had nothing but his own cloak to give. So he cut it in half, giving part to the beggar, and wrapping the rest around himself. That night, Martin had a dream in which Jesus appeared wearing half of the cloak. "Martin has given this to me", said Jesus. Soon thereafter, Martin became a Christian and grew in generosity and holiness. Today he is known as Saint Martin of Tours.

Words to Know:

Ascension

O Victor King, Lord of power and might, today you have ascended in glory above the heavens. Do not leave us orphans, but send us the Father's promised gift, the Spirit of truth. Alleluia.   (Ascension, Evening Prayer Antiphon)

Q. 61 *What did Jesus Christ do after his Resurrection?*
After his Resurrection, Jesus Christ remained on earth forty days. Then he ascended to Heaven, where he sits at the right hand of God the Father almighty.

Q. 62 *Why did Jesus Christ remain on earth forty days after his Resurrection?*
Jesus Christ remained on earth forty days after his Resurrection in order to show that he had really and truly risen from the dead, to confirm his disciples in their faith in him, and to instruct them more profoundly in his teaching.

PART THREE

God the Holy Spirit, The Sanctifier

CHAPTER 23

The Giver of Life

After the Ascension, the apostles returned to the upstairs room where they were staying in Jerusalem. They were willing to obey the command of Jesus and preach the gospel to the world, but they did not know where to start. What would they say to people? How should they travel, separately or in a group? What would they do if the Temple leaders tried to arrest them? Most of all, they wondered how they could teach in a way that would really move the hearts of the people, and convince them to receive Baptism.

The apostles knew there was only one thing to do—wait. That was what Jesus had said, "Stay in the city until you are clothed with power from on high" (Lk 24:49). That power would be the Holy Spirit, of whom Jesus had spoken many times. "He will teach you all things, and make you remember all that I have told you."

So the apostles gathered with the other followers of Jesus and stayed indoors for nine days, praying constantly. Mary, the Mother of Jesus, was with them too. They chose a new apostle to replace Judas: Matthias was his name. During that time they prayed for the coming of the Holy Spirit. On the tenth day, the sound of a roaring wind filled the house. Tongues as of fire appeared and came to rest upon their heads. The Holy Spirit had come. The apostles lost all fear of punishment and death. Their one burning desire was to proclaim the Good News. They rushed out of the house, and found a ready-made audience: the people of Jerusalem had heard the roar of wind coming from the house and had gathered there to see what was going on. The apostles began preaching, and those listening were amazed. Many of them were Jews from foreign lands, visiting Jerusalem for the feast of Pentecost. Yet each of them heard the apostles preach in his own language: Greek, Latin, Arabic, and more. This gift of tongues was given to the apostles by the Holy Spirit.

Then Peter stood up and explained to the people that this was the work of the Holy Spirit. He proclaimed that Jesus had risen from the dead and was truly the promised Messiah. Through Jesus' death, said Peter, the grace of salvation and the gifts of the Holy Spirit were available to everyone in Baptism.

Moved by Peter's words, three thousand people received Baptism that day. And so the Church of Christ made its beginning. Every year we celebrate this day on the feast of Pentecost. The word "pentecost" means "fifty days". The Holy Spirit came down upon the apostles fifty days after the Resurrection of Jesus. The Jews celebrated their feast of Pentecost as the fiftieth day after Passover. Now the Church had both a new Passover—the death and Resurrection of Jesus—

"I believe in the Holy Spirit. . . ."

and a new Pentecost—the coming of the Holy Spirit. Pentecost is the birthday of the Church.

The Holy Spirit

Who is the Holy Spirit? The Holy Spirit is God, the third Person of the Blessed Trinity. He is equal with the Father and the Son. It can be hard for us to think about the Holy Spirit. The words "Father" and "Son" give us human images to think about. The Holy Spirit is represented at times by the symbol of a dove or of fire, but these things don't tell us much about him.

Church teachings have explained that the Holy Spirit is actually the Love that God the Father and God the Son have for one another. This Love is so perfect and so great that it is another Person, equal to the Father and Son.

God Sends His Spirit

The Holy Spirit fills our souls at Baptism, and again in a more special way at Confirmation. With the Divine Love of God within us, we are able to love God and neighbor. "Do you not know" said Saint Paul "that you are God's temple and that God's Spirit dwells in you?" (1 Cor 3:16).

In the New Testament the Holy Spirit is given different names that help describe him. At different places in the Gospels Jesus refers to the Holy Spirit as the Spirit of Truth, the Comforter, and the Sanctifier. These names all remind us that the Holy Spirit is God's special gift to us. He comes to us with the gifts of wisdom, knowledge of truth, strength in our faith (that is what comfort means), and sanctity (holiness).

Besides living in each of us, the Holy Spirit is at work in the Church today. Ever since the first Pentecost, the Holy Spirit has been guiding the Church. The Spirit reminded the apostles of everything Jesus taught, so that they could teach without making any error. Whenever a problem came up in the early Church, the Holy Spirit guided the apostles to find the right solution. This divine guidance was needed even more after the apostles died, because later false teachers came with their own ideas of what Christians ought to believe. Whenever Christians needed to know what the truth really was, they had only to turn to the bishops of the Church. As successors to the apostles, bishops under the leadership of Peter's successor, the Pope, had the power to teach and defend the true faith.

The Holy Spirit is at work in Christ's Church in many ways. He inspires and prompts both individual Christians and the Church as a whole to proclaim the Good News of Jesus. He may inspire the Pope to give an important message to the world. He may inspire your bishop to open a school for handicapped children. He can move your parents to pray that their children will be saints. He can prompt you to encourage a friend to come to church with you. All these and more are actions of the Holy Spirit in our world.

Words to Know:

Pentecost   Sanctifier   Comforter

We believe in the Holy Spirit, who is Lord and Giver of life, who is adored and glorified, together with the Father and the Son. He spoke to us by the prophets; he was sent by Christ after his Resurrection and his Ascension to the Father; he illuminates, vivifies, protects, and guides the Church; he purifies the Church's members if they do not shun his grace. His action, which penetrates to the inmost of the soul, enables man to respond to the call of Jesus: "Be perfect as your Heavenly Father is perfect" (Mt 5:48).

(Credo of the People of God)

Come, Holy Spirit, Creator blest,
And in our souls take up your rest;
Come with your grace and heavenly aid
To fill the hearts which you have made.

O Comforter, to you we cry,
O heavenly Gift of God Most High,
O fount of life and fire of love,
And sweet anointing from above.

CHAPTER 24

The Mystical Body

We call Pentecost Sunday the birthday of the Church. But just as an unborn child comes to life within its mother long before birth, the Church "came to life" before Pentecost, while Jesus still walked the earth. That is because Jesus was the *Founder* of the Church.

How did Jesus found his Church? First, he called twelve of his apostles to share his life

and mission in a more special way than the others who believed in him. "Come follow me and I will make you fishers of men" (Mt 4:19).

Jesus carefully explained his message to these apostles. He gave them extra instruction that others did not receive. Jesus also gave the Twelve a chance to practice preaching the Good News. He used to send them ahead into towns and villages to prepare the people for his coming visits. He gave them the power to heal the sick and to cast out devils.

From among the Twelve, Jesus chose Peter to be leader of all:

> You are Peter and on this rock I will build my Church. And the jaws of death shall not prevail against it. I will entrust to you the keys of the Kingdom of Heaven. Whatever you declare bound on earth shall be bound in Heaven. (Mt 16:18–19)

Peter became the first Pope, the supreme teacher and leader of the whole Church.

The Mystical Body of Christ

Another name for the Church is the Mystical Body of Christ. "Mystical" means it is not a physical body, but a spiritual one. The Church is Christ's presence in the world. Through Baptism, each of us becomes joined to Christ. We are united so closely to him that we can compare this unity to the way the parts of a body are joined together.

Christ is the head of the Mystical Body. The Holy Spirit is the soul of the Mystical Body. Just as our own bodies cannot live and act without our souls, so the Holy Spirit gives the life of sanctifying grace to the Church.

As for the rest of us, we are the members, or parts, of Christ's Mystical Body. Like the parts of your own body, we "parts" of Christ's Body have many different jobs to do. Using this idea of the Church as a body Saint Paul told the early Christians to be happy with the job God gave to each of them and not to envy the job of someone else:

> It was in one Spirit that all of us, whether Jew or Greek, slave or free, were baptized into one body. All of us have been given to drink of the one Spirit. Now the body is not one member; it is many. If the foot should say, "Because I am not a hand I do not belong to the body", would it then no longer belong to the body? If the ear should say, "Because I am not an eye I do not belong to the body", would it then no longer belong to the body? If the body were all eye, what would happen to our hearing? If it were all ear, what would happen to our smelling? As it is, God has set each member of the body in the place he wanted it to be. If all the members were alike, where would the body be? There are, indeed, many different members, but one body. The eye cannot say to the hand, "I do not need you", any more than the head can say to the feet, "I do not need you." (1 Cor 12:13—21)

The True Church

By now you know that there are other churches, which are not part of the Catholic Church. These other Christian churches started years ago. At certain times in history, some Christians misunderstood some teaching of the Catholic Church or some part of the Bible. They started their own church, which they believed had the true faith. These people did not understand that Jesus promised to keep his Church free from error until the end of the world. Christians who are not Catholic share much of our faith. All Christians love and respect God's Word as it comes to us in the Bible. All believe in Jesus Our Savior. But only the Catholic Church has the whole faith. We should pray that one day all Christians will be joined together in one faith.

The Communion of Saints

We have been speaking about the Church on earth. But faithful members of Christ's Mystical Body do not leave it when they die. Those in Heaven still belong to the Church, and they help the Church by praying for God's people on earth. Souls in Purgatory are not yet with God in Heaven, but while they are waiting they also are able to pray for us. We can help them, too. Our prayers and sacrifices will shorten their time in Purgatory. When the souls for whom we have prayed reach Heaven, they will be happy to repay us by praying for us.

As you can see, all the members of Christ's Church, whether on earth, in Heaven, or in Purgatory are joined together in friendship and

"I believe . . . in the Holy Catholic Church, the Communion of Saints. . . ."

a desire to help one another. This is what we mean when we say in the Creed, "I believe in the Communion of Saints."

Q. 63 *What is the Church?*

The Church is the community of true Christians, that is, baptized persons who profess the faith and teaching of Jesus Christ, who participate in his sacraments, and who obey the pastors whom he has appointed.

Q. 64 *By whom was the Church founded?*

The Church was founded by Jesus Christ, who gathered his faithful followers into one community, placed it under the direction of the apostles with Saint Peter as its head, and gave it its Sacrifice, its sacraments, and the Holy Spirit, who gives it life.

Q. 65 *Why did Jesus Christ institute the Church?*

Jesus Christ instituted the Church so that men might have in it a secure *guide* and the *means* of holiness and eternal salvation.

Q. 66 *Why are the faithful in the Church called "saints"?*

The faithful who belong to the Church are called *saints* because they are consecrated to God, justified or sanctified by the sacraments, and they are obliged to live as holy persons.

Q. 67 *What does "Communion of Saints" mean?*

The *Communion of Saints* means that all the faithful, who form one single body in Jesus Christ, share in all the good that *exists* and *is done* in this same body, namely, in the universal Church.

Q. 68 *Do the blessed in Heaven and the souls in Purgatory form a part of the Communion of Saints?*

The blessed in Heaven and the souls in Purgatory do form a part of the Communion of Saints because they are joined to each other and with us by charity, because those in Heaven receive our prayers, and those in Purgatory our assistance, and because they all repay us with their intercession with God on our behalf.

CHAPTER 25

The Identity of the Church

Four Marks

"Go", said the golden fairy to the girl. "Only you can find the prince and break the spell that he is under. When you find him, he will not look the way you expect him to look. Because of the spell, he does not know his true identity, and so he will not be able to tell you who he is."

"Then tell me, your ladyship, however shall I know the prince from any other boy when I find him?"

"I will give you three signs by which you shall know him. Learn these signs well. . . ."

***

If you have ever read fairy tales, you know that many of them are like this. The same is true of adventure stories, where the hero must find a treasure by following signs on a map or solve a mystery by hunting for clues. Even in everyday life we reach our goal by looking for signs. "You'll know which house is mine", says a friend, "because it's the only one on the street with a red roof and white fence."

There are many religions and many churches in the world. How is someone able to discover which is the true faith revealed by God? How are you able to know what makes the Catholic Church different from any other?

The Catholic Church has four special signs

that mark it off from all others. We call these signs the marks of the Church. We repeat the four marks when we say the Nicene Creed at Mass: "We believe in *one*, *holy*, *catholic*, and *apostolic* Church." Let us look at these signs one by one.

The Church is one: All Catholics in the world share the exact same beliefs about God, the Redemption, the sacraments, the Blessed Virgin Mary, and what is right and wrong. Catholics may belong to different *rites*, which have different liturgies and customs, but we all believe in the same truths of our salvation. You will not find this "oneness" or unity in other Christian churches. In those churches, beliefs of the members will vary from one person to another.

The Church is holy: First of all, this does

not mean that all Catholics are holy. Just as there are good and bad people, there are good and bad Catholics. But the Church is holy, because Jesus, who founded it, and the Holy Spirit, who guides it, are holy. The teaching of the Church is holy, and its aim is to make its members holy. The Church is so concerned about making us holy that it gives us special helps, called sacraments.

To prove that the Church's plan to make us holy really "works", we only have to look at the many Catholic saints. Thousands of men, women, and children from all walks of life were able to become holy through the help of the Church. Learning about the saints and making friends with them is another aid to help us reach Heaven.

The Church is catholic: The word "catholic" means universal or for all. The Church has spread to every nation on earth. No one has to have a certain nationality or special customs in order to feel at home in the Church. Despite their differences of geography, customs, clothing, language, and skin color, all Catholics are united in the brotherhood of faith.

The Church is apostolic: Our spiritual leaders, the Pope and the bishops, can trace their powers all the way back to the apostles. Each one received his powers from another bishop, who in turn received his powers from another. The line is unbroken throughout the Church's history. Because of this, the bishops, with the Pope as their head, can teach as the apostles taught, with the guidance of the Holy Spirit.

Symbols of the Church

The New Testament gives us many symbols, or word pictures, to tell us about the Church. We have already talked about one of them: the Church as the Mystical Body of Christ. One symbol Jesus often used was the shepherd and sheep. Jesus called himself the Good Shepherd, who lays down his life to save his sheep from the wolves. The Church is the sheepfold. (See Jn 10:1 – 18.) Jesus also called Peter a shepherd, when he told him, "Feed my lambs. . . . Feed my sheep" (Jn 21:15 – 16).

Jesus also compared the Church to a vineyard. "I am the vine, and you are the branches", Jesus told his apostles. "He who abides in me, and I in him, will bear much fruit" (Jn 15:5).

Later on, the Church was also called the Bark (ship) of Peter. The Church is like a great ship, steered by the Pope. Those who are on board the ship are safe from the stormy waters

---

PRAYER FOR UNITY OF THE CHURCH

Almighty and merciful God, you willed that the different nations should become one people through your Son. Grant, in your kindness, that those who glory in being known as Christians may put aside their differences and become one in truth and charity and that all men, enlightened by the true faith, may be united in fraternal communion in one Church. Through Christ Our Lord. *Amen.*

of sin and disbelief. From time to time someone may fall ''overboard'' through mortal sin,
but the Church throws him a ''lifeline'': the
sacrament of Penance.

Q. 69   *Which is the Church of Jesus Christ?*

The Church of Jesus Christ subsists in the Roman Catholic Church, because it alone is *one*, *holy*, *catholic*, and *apostolic*, as he himself willed it to be.

Q. 70   *Why is the Church one?*

The Church is one because all of its members always have had, now have, and always will have the same faith, the same Sacrifice, the same sacraments, and the same visible head, the Roman Pontiff, who is the Successor of Saint Peter. Thus they all together form one single body, the Mystical Body of Jesus Christ.

Q. 71   *Why is the Church holy?*

The Church is holy because Jesus Christ, its invisible head, and the Spirit who gives it life, are holy; because its doctrine, its Sacrifice and its sacraments are holy; because all of its members are called to make themselves holy; and because many members actually were holy, are holy now, and will be holy in the future.

Q. 72   *Why is the Church catholic?*

The Church is catholic, that is, universal, because it was instituted for all men, is suitable for all men, and has been extended over the whole world.

Q. 73   *Why is the Church apostolic?*

The Church is apostolic because it has been founded upon the apostles and on their preaching, and because it is governed by their successors, the legitimate pastors, who continue to transmit both doctrine and power without interruption or change.

CHAPTER 26

The Church Rules

The Church is holy and *divine* because it was founded by Jesus, who is God. But the Church is also human. Its members are redeemed by Christ and are striving for holiness, but they are not perfect. Even the early Christians were not able to work together in perfect agreement. For instance, the Greek Christians complained that their widows were getting less of the money collected for the poor than widows of the Hebrew Christians. Another

problem came up when pagans who became Christians refused to follow certain laws of the Jewish religion. They did not think that these laws had anything to do with belief in Jesus. The Jewish Christians, on the other hand, thought just the opposite. After all, Jesus had not given permission for these laws to be changed. Still more difficulties arose when the Temple leaders began persecuting the Christians. Someone had to decide where and how Christ's followers should meet in secret for worship and instruction.

Fortunately, Jesus had given the apostles not only the mission to preach the gospel but the power to govern the Church as well. Peter and the apostles had the power to make decisions about running the Church in everyday matters. They could also make laws that would help Church members to live the Christian life more easily. These decisions and laws were not truths about God that could never be changed. But Christians were bound to accept these decisions because the apostles had the special authority given them by Jesus, who promised them the guidance of the Holy Spirit. Remember the words of Jesus to Saint Peter: "What you bind on earth will be bound in Heaven; what you loose on earth will be loosed in Heaven" (Mt 16:19).

The apostles were the very first *bishops*. As today, the bishop had the power to teach the message of Jesus, to govern the Christians under his care and to administer the sacraments. Each bishop was in charge of Christians in a certain part of the world. The Church grew, however, and the apostles knew they could not be everywhere at once. They also knew that they would not be with the Church on earth for ever. Since more than twelve bishops were needed, the apostles passed on their powers to other men. Through the years, these powers have been passed down, right to this very day. Today the bishop in charge of the *diocese* where you live has these same powers to rule, teach, and sanctify.

Even though there are many bishops, there are not enough to take care of every spiritual need of every Christian. That is why bishops have helpers called *priests*. Bishops share with priests their powers to celebrate the Eucharist and some of the other sacraments. Priests also help the bishop to govern, by taking care of smaller groups of Catholics, which we know as *parishes*. The priest is also allowed to represent his bishop's teaching authority by preaching at Mass.

Priests also have helpers who are called *deacons*. Like the priest, the deacon is *ordained* by a bishop, but he does not have the power to celebrate the Eucharist. The deacon can administer the sacrament of Baptism; he can witness marriages. The deacon may proclaim the Gospel and preach at Mass and distribute Holy Communion. He can also conduct funeral services. The deacon helps the priest by visiting the sick and by using his talents in different ways for the good of the parish.

Saint Peter was the first bishop of Rome. He was also the first *Pope*. The Pope has the power to govern and teach the entire Church. Whenever a Pope dies, a new one is elected from a special group of Church leaders called *Cardinals*. The Pope, often with the help of the bishops, makes laws that govern the entire Church. One example of Church laws that govern Catholics the world over are the "Precepts of the Church". By these precepts every Catholic must:

---

1. Assist at Mass on all Sundays and Holy Days of Obligation.
2. Fast and abstain on the days appointed.
3. Confess his sins at least once a year. (Annual confession is obligatory only if serious sin is involved.)
4. Receive Holy Communion during the Easter time.
5. Contribute to the support of the Church.
6. Observe the laws of the Church concerning marriage.

Because Christ gave it the mission to govern his followers, the Church can change according to the needs of God's children. Over the years, some Church laws about fasting, the liturgy,

---

"And I tell you, you are Peter, and on this rock I will build my Church, and the powers of death shall not prevail against it. I will give you the keys of the Kingdom of Heaven, and whatever you bind on earth shall be bound in Heaven, and whatever you loose on earth shall be loosed in Heaven."

(Matthew 16:18−19)

and the sacraments have changed. But the Church also tells us what things cannot be changed: those things which God has revealed as true. This second mission of the Church, to *teach*, will be the topic of the next chapter.

Words to Know:

diocese   bishop   cardinal

Q. 74 *Who are the legitimate pastors of the Church?*
The legitimate pastors of the Church are the Pope, who is the Supreme Pontiff, and the bishops united with him.

Q. 75 *Who is the Pope?*
The Pope is the Successor of Saint Peter in the See of Rome and in the primacy, namely, in the universal apostolate and episcopal power. Therefore he is the visible head of the entire Church, the Vicar of Jesus Christ, who is the invisible head; hence this Church is called the Roman Catholic Church.

CHAPTER 27

Teach All Nations

Maybe you have played a game called "telephone". About a dozen people line up, and the first makes up a "message". He whispers that message in the ear of the second person, who then whispers to the next person, and so on down the line. The fun comes when the last player in line says out loud the message he has received. Usually it is a very silly mixed-up sentence. The only way to find out what the real message was, is to ask the first player, who made up the message to begin with.

If it had not been for the guidance of the Holy Spirit, the message Jesus gave to mankind might also have become confused and mixed-up. No one has a perfect mind or memory. As the years went by, mistakes might have crept into the early Christians' knowledge of their faith, and important things could have been left out. Worse still, there have been times throughout the Church's history when certain people tried to change the faith on purpose, to suit their own ideas of what was true.

But Christ wanted to keep his Church safe from error. He wanted his Church to be able to proclaim the truth with certainty. So he gave his apostles and their successors the mission to *teach*. "Teach them to observe all that I have commanded you" (Mt 28:20): this was one of the last things Jesus said to his apostles before the Ascension. After the Ascension, Jesus sent the Holy Spirit to help them know perfectly what Jesus wanted them to teach. "He will teach you all things, and bring to your memory all that I have said to you" (Jn 14:26). "When the Spirit of truth comes, he will guide you into all truth" (Jn 16:13).

Peter and the apostles passed their teaching authority on to the Pope and bishops who came after them. Then they, too, had the power to *interpret* (to explain) *Sacred Scripture* and *Sacred Tradition*. Scripture, as you know, is the written Word of God. We also call Scripture the *Bible*. The Old Testament of the Bible contains the books about the history of creation and of God's chosen people. The New Testament contains the Gospels and writings of the early Church. But during the first years of the Church there was no "Bible", no one book of writings that made up God's written word. This was one of the first big tasks of the teaching Church: to decide which Jewish writings and which of the many writings about Jesus were really *inspired* by God and should belong to Sacred Scripture.

Sacred Tradition means everything that was handed on to us from the apostles. It includes the preaching, example, and Christian way of life of the apostles. All this they themselves had received—from the teaching of Jesus, from the example of his life and works, and from the inspiration of the Holy Spirit.

The teaching Church is needed to explain

with the Pope to make decisions about how to teach and govern the Church. Many Councils have been held in the history of the Church. The last one was the Second Vatican Council, held from 1963 to 1965.

Each bishop is the spiritual father and chief teacher in his own diocese. The Pope is the spiritual father and teacher of all Catholics the world over. We all must believe the Pope when he teaches us in matters of faith and morals, knowing that the Holy Spirit is speaking through him. This is the meaning of the expression: "Where Peter is, there too is the Church".

All Nations

The Church is not content to teach its truth only to those who are already Catholic. Since Jesus died for all men, the Church tries to bring his saving message to every part of the world. Although the Church has grown tremendously since the times of the apostles, there are still people who have never heard of Jesus. There are many others who have heard of him, but do not understand or do not have the gift of faith. The Church reaches out to all these peoples, in the hope "that all may be one" (Jn 17:21).

The task of preaching the gospel to those outside the Church is called evangelization. Brave men and women called *missionaries* go to distant lands in order to bring the people to Christ. In a spirit of love and compassion they do their best to feed the hungry, heal the sick, and educate the children. They know that a big part of spreading the gospel is *living* the gospel. "As often as you did it for one of my least brothers, you did it for me" (Mt 25:40).

The work of evangelization can take place in our own country, our own town, and maybe, even our own families. You can share in this work by praying for those who are outside the Church, by giving money to the missions, and by doing your best to express the Good News

Scripture and Tradition to Christians. Some parts of the Bible are difficult to understand, and different people will explain them in different ways. The Pope and bishops with him have the guidance of the Holy Spirit in explaining the Bible to us. They also have the Spirit's guidance in teaching us the truths that come from Sacred Tradition.

When the Pope, as head of the Church on earth, teaches all Catholics about some truth of faith (what we must believe) or morals (how Christians must act), he is *infallible*. Infallible means protected from all error by the Holy Spirit. The bishops are infallible when, in union with the Pope, they teach something on faith and morals which must be held by all Catholics as definitively true. This happens in a special way when the Church holds an Ecumenical Council. At an Ecumenical Council, all of the bishops from around the world meet in your daily life. People can learn about the Christian way of life by watching how you live. You can teach your friends by speaking freely about your faith when the conversation turns to religion.

In a parable, Our Lord compared the world to a rich vineyard. "The harvest is great," he said, "but the laborers are few." Millions of souls are waiting for the truth that will bring them eternal happiness. Each of us can help them in some way. Ask God how you can help with the "harvest".

Words to Know:

infallibility   Tradition   evangelization

"Full authority has been given to me both in Heaven and on earth; go, therefore, and make disciples of all the nations. Baptize them in the name of the Father, and of the Son, and of the Holy Spirit. Teach them to carry out everything I have commanded you. And know that I am with you always, until the end of the world!"

(Matthew 28:19—20)

Q. 76 *What do the Pope and the bishops united with him constitute?*

The Pope and the bishops united with him constitute the *teaching* Church, that is, the one that has received from Jesus Christ the mission of *teaching* the truths and laws of God to all men. And men receive *only* from this teaching Church the *full* and *secure* knowledge that is necessary to live in a Christian manner.

Q. 77 *Can the teaching Church err in teaching the truths revealed by God?*

The teaching Church cannot err in teaching the truths revealed by God: it is infallible, because "the Spirit of truth" (Jn 15:26), as promised by Jesus Christ, assists it continually.

Q. 78 *Can the Pope, taken separately, err in teaching the truths revealed by God?*

The Pope, taken separately, cannot err in teaching the truths revealed by God; that is, he is *infallible* just as the Church is, when, as *pastor and teacher of all Christians*, he *defines* doctrines on *faith* and *morals*.

CHAPTER 28

Called to Holiness

Christians are children of God. But what does that mean? To find out what it means to be a child of God, we must think about what it means to be a child of human parents. First, and most important, our parents give us life; without them we would never have been born. Then, they care for the children they have brought into the world; feeding us, clothing us, caring for us when we are sick or hurt, and preparing us for adulthood. These are all ways that parents express their love for their children.

God, our Heavenly Father, cares for the needs of our souls just as parents care for the health of our bodies. We are born as God's children at Baptism. Our souls are fed by sanctifying grace, which we receive from all of the sacraments, but the greatest spiritual food is the Holy Eucharist. When our souls are sick and injured by sin, God heals them through the sacrament of Penance. We are strengthened for adulthood in the Church by the sacrament of Confirmation.

The seven sacraments are like seven fountains of grace which come to us in the Church. Each sacrament was *instituted* (begun) by Christ to bring to souls the new life of grace he won for us on the Cross. A sacrament is a *visible sign*: although we cannot see grace, we can see the things God uses to give us grace. Things such as water, bread and wine, holy oil, the priest, and spoken words all help us to understand what the sacraments do.

Some people may say, ''I thought that Jesus died to free us from sin and gave us grace. So why do we need sacraments to do the same thing?'' Such a question misses the point. The sacraments are not something that we need in addition to Christ's dying for us. Jesus gave us the sacraments so we could have a sure way to receive the grace that he won for us.

The Church has the mission *to sanctify*, that is to make her members holy. She does this first of all by the sacrament of Baptism. Baptism removes original sin and fills our souls with sanctifying grace. A newly baptized soul is holy and pleasing to God. Unfortunately, this perfect holiness may not last for ever. Although Baptism removes original sin, it does not remove all the *effects* (results) of original sin. And one of these effects is a strong inclination to sin. That means we fall into sin very easily. Sins that we ourselves commit are called ''actual sins''.

Imagine someone who has had a terrible disease. Finally, he is cured, but for the rest of his life he is not a very strong person, and he often catches cold. Original sin is like the disease. Baptism ''cures'' it, but our souls are left weak, and we often fall into actual sin.

There are two kinds of actual sin: mortal and venial. Mortal sin destroys the life of grace

"I believe . . . in the forgiveness of sins. . . ."

within us. By committing mortal sin we destroy our life with God. A soul that dies in mortal sin cannot receive eternal life in Heaven. Three things are needed in order for a sin to be mortal. First, it must be a very serious matter. Second, the person must really know that it is serious. Third, the person must commit the sin on purpose. A good example is missing Sunday Mass. This is a serious matter. But if someone had never been taught that it is a serious matter, he would not be committing a mortal sin by missing Mass. Nor would he sin mortally if he knew it, but he was too sick to go to Mass or he had no way of getting there. In those cases, he would not be missing Mass on purpose.

Venial sin is a less serious sin. We are still in God's friendship and love even though we are in a state of venial sin. Still, venial sins offend God. Venial sins hurt other people and ourselves. If we do not try to keep away from venial sin, we may soon find ourselves committing mortal sins as well. Jesus suffered pain and sadness from our venial sins as well as from our mortal sins.

Jesus knew that even after Baptism, Christians would still sin. He wanted there to be a way for them to receive God's forgiveness again and again. He wanted his followers to have special help in overcoming sin in their daily lives. And so Jesus instituted the sacrament of Penance. He gave his apostles the power to forgive sins in his name: "Whose sins you forgive, they are forgiven them." The apostles later passed on this power to forgive sins. When we receive the sacrament of Penance, the sanctifying grace we have lost through mortal sin is restored to our souls.

Ordinarily we may not receive the Holy Eucharist if we have an unconfessed mortal sin. Receiving the Eucharist in the state of mortal sin would itself be another mortal sin. It is all right to receive the Eucharist when there are venial sins on our souls; in fact, receiving the Eucharist can remove our venial sins. However, it is good to confess venial sins. Frequent Confession will give us the grace to avoid both mortal and venial sin. Receiving the sacrament of Penance often (once a month is a good idea) will make us better and stronger Christians.

"You, therefore, must be perfect, as your Heavenly Father is perfect."
(Matthew 5:41)

How to Make the Most of The Sacrament of Penance

If you were hurt and needed to see the doctor, you would do your best to help the doctor make you well again. On the way to his office, you would think of what you wanted to say to him. You would carefully answer his questions about how you had been injured and where you felt the pain. You would carefully follow his instructions about taking any special medicine or keeping the bandages clean. And if the injury was caused partly through your own fault, you would promise yourself to be more careful in the future.

In order to make a good Confession, we should treat our injured souls the same way. Here are the five steps needed to make a good Confession.

1. *Examination of conscience*: this means to think deeply and get a clear idea of what sins you have committed, and how many times you have committed them. It helps to pray to the Holy Spirit for help in remembering.

2. *Be sorry for sin*: remember that each of your sins helped to crucify Jesus. Think, too, of how your sins may have hurt others. Tell God you are sorry and pray the Act of Contrition.

3. *Make up your mind not to sin again*: and decide what steps you will take to avoid these same sins in the future.

4. *Confess your sins to the priest*: If after you leave church, you remember that you forgot to tell one of your sins do not worry about it. If the sin was mortal, tell the priest the next time you receive the sacrament. If venial, there is no need to do this.

5. *Do the penance the priest gives you*: The penance the priest gives may be some prayers or a specific action. Doing the penance shows that you are serious about wanting to overcome

sin. It helps in a small way to make up for sin, by balancing the evil you have done with something that is good. You should do your penance as soon as you can.

Q. 79 *What are the means of holiness and of eternal salvation that are found in the Church?*

The means of holiness and of eternal salvation which are found in the Church are the true faith, the Sacrifice, and the sacraments, together with mutual spiritual aids, such as prayer, spiritual counsel, and good example.

Q. 80 *Are the means of holiness and eternal salvation common to all men?*

The means of holiness and eternal salvation are common to all men who belong to the Church, that is, to the *faithful*. In the apostolic writings, the faithful are called ''the *saints*''. For this reason, their union with each other and their participation in these means is a *communion of the saints* in holy things.

Q. 81 *What are the sacraments?*

The sacraments are efficacious signs of grace instituted by Jesus Christ to make us holy.

Q. 82 *Who gave to the sacraments the power of conferring grace?*

Jesus Christ, true God and true man, gave the sacraments the power of conferring grace, which he himself merited for us by his Passion and death.

Q. 83 *How do the sacraments make us holy?*

The sacraments make us holy either by giving us the first sanctifying grace, which takes away sin, or by increasing that grace which we already possess.

Q. 84 *What does the "forgiveness of sins" mean?*

"Forgiveness of sins" means that Jesus Christ gave to the apostles and to their successors the power of forgiving every sin in the Church.

Q. 85 *How are sins forgiven in the Church?*

Sins are forgiven in the Church principally by the sacraments of Baptism and Penance, which were instituted by Jesus Christ for this purpose.

Q. 86 *What is sin?*

Sin is an offense done to God by disobeying his law.

Q. 87 *How many kinds of sin are there?*

Sin is of two kinds: *original* and *actual*.

Q. 88 *What is original sin?*

Original sin is the sin which mankind committed in Adam, its first parent, and which every human being receives from Adam through natural descent.

Q. 89 *How is original sin taken away?*

Original sin is taken away by Holy Baptism.

Q. 90 *What is actual sin?*

Actual sin is a sin which is committed voluntarily by one who has the use of reason.

Q. 91 *In how many ways is actual sin committed?*

Actual sin is committed in four ways, in *thoughts*, in *words*, in *deeds*, and in *omissions*.

Q. 92 *How many kinds of actual sin are there?*

Actual sin is of two kinds: *mortal* and *venial*.

Q. 93 *What is mortal sin?*

Mortal sin is an act of disobedience to the law of God in a *serious matter*, done with *full knowledge* and *deliberate consent*.

Q. 94 *Why is serious sin called "mortal"?*

Serious sin is called mortal because it takes away from the soul divine grace, which is the *life* of the soul, robs the soul of its merits and of the capacity to earn new merit, and makes it worthy of everlasting punishment, eternal death in Hell.

Q. 95 *If mortal sin makes a man unable to acquire merits, is it not therefore useless for the sinner to do good works?*

It is not useless for the sinner to do good works. In fact, he is obliged to do them in order not to become worse by omitting them and falling into additional sins and in order to dispose himself by means of them, in some way, to being converted and regaining the grace of God.

Q. 96 *How does one regain the grace of God, lost by mortal sin?*

The grace of God, lost by mortal sin, is regained by a good sacramental confession or by perfect contrition, which liberates from sins even though the obligation remains of confessing them sacramentally.

Q. 97 *What is venial sin?*

Venial sin is an act of disobedience to the law of God in a lesser matter—or also in a matter in itself serious, but done without full knowledge and consent.

Q. 98 *Why is a sin which is not serious called "venial"?*

A sin which is not serious is called "venial", that is, forgivable, because it does not take grace away and because it can be forgiven by repentance and good works, even without sacramental confession.

Q. 99 *Is venial sin harmful to the soul?*

Yes, venial sin is harmful to the soul because it chills its love of God, disposes it for mortal sin, and makes it worthy of temporal punishments in this life and in the next.

CHAPTER 29

The Mother of God In Our Lives

The first miracle Jesus performed in his public life was unlike any other. He did not heal someone of a terrible disease or handicap. Instead he solved a little problem—so little that Jesus may not have even been thinking of doing it at first. He did it at the request of his mother, Mary.

This was the miracle at Cana, where Jesus turned water into wine at a wedding party. The newly married couple had run out of wine before the party was over. Mary, one of the wedding guests, felt sorry for the embarrassed couple. So Mary told Jesus what had happened. Jesus answered that it was not yet the right time to begin showing his miraculous powers. Mary was confident that her Son would not refuse the favor she asked. And so Jesus had the servants fill large jars with water, which he turned into the most delicious wine.

We might say Our Lady was being very ''motherly'' toward the bride and bridegroom at Cana, looking out for their needs and interceding for them. (Her request to Jesus was a kind of prayer.) Jesus must have wanted Mary to be a ''Mother'' to all his friends. That is why, as he was dying on the Cross, he told his Mother to be a Mother to his young apostle John. ''Woman, behold your son.'' We be- lieve that with these words, Jesus gave his Mother not only to John but to all Christians. And so we honor Mary today not only as Mother of God but as Mother of the Church.

Mary has an important role in our redemption. Jesus is sometimes called ''the new Adam'' because his death was the act of obedience to God that undid the disobedience of Adam. We can also call Mary ''the new Eve''. Eve helped bring sin and death to the entire human race by her unwillingness to obey God's will. Mary, by submitting perfectly to God's will all her life, helped restore what had been lost.

Mary was with the apostles at Pentecost. Her prayers helped the early Church to grow

---

We believe that Mary is the Mother, who remained ever a Virgin, of the Incarnate Word, our God and Savior Jesus Christ, and that by reason of this singular election, she was, in consideration of the merits of her Son, redeemed in a more eminent manner, preserved from all stain of original sin, and filled with the gift of grace more than all other creatures.

(Credo of the People of God)

quickly. When Mary died, she was taken into Heaven body and soul. We call this privilege the *Assumption* of Our Lady, and we celebrate it each year on August 15th.

From Heaven, Mary continues to be Mother of the Church and Mother to each of us. Remember the wedding at Cana? Our Blessed Mother is interested in our problems and needs. If we turn to her, she will gladly pray to God on our behalf. Jesus will listen to her because she is the holiest of all the saints, in addition to being his own beloved Mother.

Mary's Gift to Us

The Rosary is one of the most powerful prayers we can say. As we pray the Our Fathers and Hail Marys on the Rosary beads, we are supposed to think about certain scenes from the lives of Jesus and Mary, which are called the mysteries of the Rosary. (See the *Prayers* section at the back of the book for a list of the mysteries.) The Church has often urged families to say the Rosary together. Many parents and children have found that the family Rosary has brought much grace and happiness to their families.

Words to Know:

Assumption   Rosary

HAIL, HOLY QUEEN

Hail, holy Queen, Mother of mercy, our life, our sweetness, and our hope! To thee do we cry, poor banished children of Eve; to thee do we send up our sighs, mourning, and weeping in this valley of tears. Turn, then, most gracious Advocate, thine eyes of mercy toward us; and after this, our exile, show unto us the blessed fruit of thy womb, Jesus. O clement, O loving, O sweet Virgin Mary. *Amen*

Mary Visits Her Children

At various times in history Our Blessed Mother has appeared on earth to certain people. She does this to make our faith stronger or to give us a special message from God. These visions are not an essential part of our faith in the way that the beliefs of our Creed are. But they are good to know about, and they can help us to love Jesus and Mary more. Here are some appearances of Our Lady you should know about:

Our Lady of Guadalupe: In the year 1531, the Blessed Mother appeared to a man in Mexico. Juan Diego was an Indian who had become a Christian only a short while before. By appearing to him Our Lady showed her special love for the Indian people of the New World. When Juan Diego went to tell his bishop what had happened, a picture of Our Lady miraculously appeared on his coat. This miraculous picture can still be seen in the church of Our Lady of Guadalupe in Mexico.

Our Lady of Lourdes: In 1858, Mary appeared eighteen times to a fourteen year old girl, Bernadette Soubirous, near Lourdes, France. At the last apparition the Blessed Mother revealed her identity to Bernadette by saying, ''I am the Immaculate Conception''. This apparition of Mary was important because four years previously, in 1854, the Church had defined as a dogma the truth of the Immaculate Conception of Mary, that is, that Mary was conceived without original sin. Bernadette was canonized a saint in 1933.

Our Lady of Fatima: In 1917, three children in Fatima, Portugal, began having monthly visits from Mary. The Blessed Mother asked them to say the Rosary every day for world peace and to make sacrifices for sinners. The last time Our Lady visited the children, God gave a sign to show the people who came that the children were not lying. That day seventy thousand people saw the sun spin and fall toward the earth, then stop and return to its normal position.

The message of Fatima is important for us today. Mary promised that if enough people say the Rosary and make sacrifices, the world would be saved from war. Would you join in the peace plan from Heaven?

CHAPTER 30

Unto Everlasting Life

You may have noticed that some people—usually grownups—simply refuse to talk about, or even think about, death. If a child were to ask, "What happens when you die?" or, "Am I going to die someday?" such people would avoid answering. Instead they would reply, "Don't ask such questions. You must not think about such horrible things."

Although death is not a pleasant thing, it is not wise to run away from the thought of it. Death will come to all of us. Each day we live takes us one day closer to the day we die. Knowing and thinking about what death really means should help us to face it with less fear than those who may have refused to think about it at all.

Everything that is part of nature reaches a point when it begins to come apart or come to an end. All plants and animals die. Even things which seem to last for ever, such as rocks and mountains, slowly wear away into dust over thousands of years. Our bodies also belong to the world of nature, and one day they will die. Our souls are spirits which live for ever, but God created us to be complete persons, body and soul, and he has promised to reunite our bodies and souls so that we shall live for ever. It is normal to fear the pain of dying and to be sad over separation from those we love. But it helps to know that death is not really the end of us.

At death, we will be judged on how we made use of the grace Jesus won for us on the Cross. Those who die in the state of mortal sin, without having repented, will spend eternity in Hell. People often ask, "How can a loving God send someone to Hell?" It is incorrect to picture a poor soul being "sent " to Hell by God, dragged away while crying hopelessly for forgiveness. That is not the way it happens. When a person dies in mortal sin, his soul is for ever fixed in hatred of God and love for no one but himself. Such a soul would not even be happy in Heaven. Those who go to Hell send themselves there. Although souls in Hell do not want God, they cannot be happy without him. God is the source of all happiness; without him no one can be happy. So the worst suffering of Hell is the loss of God.

But if we die in the state of grace, we will enjoy eternity with God in Heaven. It is impossible to imagine how wonderful Heaven really is. Paintings and stories about a Heaven full of clouds and angels playing harps make Heaven seem unreal or even boring. The fact is Heaven is more real, more beautiful, and more interesting than any place on earth. If you do not like the idea of clouds and light, then think of majestic forests and mountains, or anything that you find beautiful. But remember that Heaven is not really like that either. It is far more beautiful than anything we can imagine.

It is the presence of God that keeps us for

ever happy in Heaven. We will not miss the joys of life on earth. God is the source of all that we love, so we will find in him everything that made us truly happy on earth—and more. "We shall see him as he is", says Saint John (1 Jn 3:2). At the same time, the sight of God will not cause us to ignore everyone else. On the contrary, because we will love God perfectly in Heaven, we will be able to love others better than we ever could on earth. In Heaven we will be reunited with friends and relatives who have died before us, knowing and loving them better than we ever did before. We will meet the saints and angels. At last we will see our guardian angels and recognize them as old

friends. Best of all, we will be able to know and love Jesus and Mary better than any friends we have had on earth.

Even though anyone who dies in the state of grace is saved, not all souls go straight to Heaven. If someone dies with venial sins on his soul or if he was not as sorry as he should have been for past mortal sins, then he is not quite ready for Heaven. Such a soul still has to be cleansed until it loves God perfectly and has no trace of sin left. So these souls go to Purgatory for awhile. In Purgatory, souls will be purified of all that kept them from being close to God while on earth. These souls are suffering for having wasted time during life that could have been spent growing closer to God. At the same time, they are filled with hope. That is because they know Heaven will be theirs soon.

It should comfort us to know there is a place like Purgatory. Thanks to Purgatory, we know that if we have tried to love and serve God, even though we could have loved him much more, we will not go to Heaven unprepared. You would not want to go to a party in an old, dirty dress or play in the Little League championship without a uniform. Purgatory will not be fun, but it will make us ready for Heaven.

It is also good to know that we can help the souls in Purgatory. When we pray for them or cheerfully offer up some unpleasant thing that happens to us their stay in Purgatory can be shortened. This is one reason why we offer prayers and the Mass for the dead, especially for those from our own families.

The End of This World

When in God's infinite wisdom it is the right time, the world will come to an end. This is not a thing to be feared. The end of the world will bring the return of Jesus to earth, this time as

"I believe . . . in the resurrection of the body and life everlasting. . . ."

the triumphant and glorious King of Heaven. He will judge the living and the dead, so that all of us can see the good God has done in each of our lives and in the whole human race.

The end of the world will also be the time for "the resurrection of the body", in which we express our belief when we say the Creed. Except for Mary, human beings in Heaven now are not complete: part of them is missing. But in the end, God will make our bodies new and strong again, and reunite them with our souls. Then our joy in Heaven will be even greater. We will be able to enjoy the happiness of Heaven with both our souls and our bodies. Our bodies will be beautiful and perfect in every way, like the body of Jesus after his Resurrection. Saint John had a vision of the end of the world, and he tried to put it into words:

> I saw a new Heaven and a new earth; for the first Heaven and the first earth had passed away, and the sea was no more. . . .
>
> And I heard a great voice from the throne saying, "Behold, the dwelling of God is with men. He will dwell with them. . . ."

He will wipe away every tear from their eyes, and death shall be no more, neither shall there be mourning nor crying nor pain any more, for the former things have passed away. (Rev 21:1—4)

All of us long for perfect happiness. Perfect joy will be ours if we use this life to get ourselves ready for it. Heaven is our true home; earth is just our journey to find it. Every prayer we say, every sacrament we receive, every act of love for others makes us more and more into the kind of person who will be able to enjoy eternity with God. We call this kind of person a "saint" even if he or she has not been officially named a saint by the Church. All of us want to "be something" someday: a priest, a nun, a doctor, a teacher, a parent, or even the president. But there is nothing better or more exciting to wish for than to be a saint. We can start making that wish come true right now.

Words to Know:

resurrection of the body   eternal life
General Judgment   Particular Judgment

Q. 100 *Will Jesus Christ ever return to this earth in a visible manner?*

Jesus Christ will return visibly to this earth at the end of the world to judge the living and the dead—that is, all men, good and evil.

Q. 101 *Will Jesus Christ wait until the end of the world to judge us?*

Jesus Christ will not wait until the end of the world to judge us, but will judge each one of us immediately after death.

Q. 102 *Are there two Judgments?*

Yes, there are two Judgments: the one is *particular*, of each soul, immediately after death; the other is *general*, of all men, at the end of the world.

Q. 103 *On what will Jesus Christ judge us?*

Jesus Christ will judge us on the good and evil that we have done in life, including our thoughts and the things we failed to do.

Q. 104 *After the Particular Judgment, what happens to the soul?*

After the Particular Judgment, if it is without sin and without a debt of punishment for sin, the soul goes into Heaven. If it has some venial sin or temporal punishment for sin, it goes into Purgatory until it has made satisfaction. If it is in mortal sin, as a changeless rebel against God, it goes into Hell.

Q. 105 *What is Purgatory?*

Purgatory is the *temporary* suffering of the lack of the vision of God and of other punishments, which remove from the soul the remains of sin, making it worthy of seeing God.

Q. 106 *Can we help and even liberate souls from the pains of Purgatory?*

We can help and even liberate souls from the pains of Purgatory with good works—our prayers, indulgences, alms, and other good works, especially by means of the Holy Mass.

Q. 107 *Is it certain that Heaven and Hell exist?*

Yes, it is certain that Heaven and Hell exist: God has revealed this, frequently promising eternal life and the enjoyment of him himself to the good and threatening the wicked with damnation and eternal fire.

Q. 108 *How long will Heaven and Hell last?*

Heaven and Hell will last for ever.

Q. 109 *What awaits us at the end of life?*

The sorrows and the decay of death and the Particular Judgment await us at the end of this life.

Q. 110 *What awaits us at the end of the world?*

The resurrection of the body and the General Judgment await us at the end of the world.

Q. 111 *What does ''resurrection of the body'' mean?*

The *resurrection of the body* means that our body will be reconstituted and reunited to our soul, by the power of God, in order to participate during eternal life in the reward or punishment which the soul has merited.

Q. 112 *What does eternal life mean?*

Eternal life means that the reward, like the punishment, will last for ever and that the vision of God will be the true life and happiness of the soul, while being deprived of him will be the greatest unhappiness, like an eternal death.

Q. 113 *What does the word ''Amen'' mean?*

The word *Amen* means *truly*, or *so it is*, or *so let it be*. With this word we confirm as true all that we profess in the Creed, hoping for the remission of our sins, our resurrection in glory, and eternal life with God.

Appendix

Celebrating The Church Year

The Church has divided the calendar into holy seasons which celebrate the history of our salvation. With each season, there are changes in the prayers and readings of the liturgy and the colors of the priest's vestments. Faithful Christians also have special customs as the holy seasons change. For instance, there is the Advent wreath and its prayers in preparation for Christmas, sacrifices during Lent in memory of Our Lord's sufferings, and praying the Rosary during the months of October and May in honor of Our Blessed Mother.

Within each season, there are days set aside to honor events in salvation history and events in the life of Our Blessed Mother. There are also many days in the Church year set aside in memory of the saints. That is because the Church wishes to take notice of certain men, women, boys, and girls who were ordinary people like us, yet who learned to love God in an extraordinary way. And since everyone in Heaven is a saint, even those who have not been canonized by the Church, there is a special feast day for all of them, too. It is All Saints' Day, on November 1.

The feasts of the Church vary in importance. Easter, Pentecost, and Christmas are among the greatest Holy Days in the Church year.

Each country's bishops decide which days are Holy Days of Obligation: that is, days on which all Catholics must attend Mass.

It is a good idea to look at a Catholic calendar to keep track of the many feasts and saints' days. The word "holiday" means holy day, and we can celebrate many Church holidays all year round. There may be some saints that you especially like or wish to learn more about, such as a saint whose name you bear. When that saint's feast comes around, attend Mass, visit the Blessed Sacrament, or say a special prayer to that saint. Read a book on that saint's life. Some families have parties for their children on the feast days of their patron saints.

Here are some of the important Holy Days of the Church year.

Solemnity of Mary, the Mother of God *(January 1):* We honor Mary because of her special privilege in being the Mother of Jesus, true God and true man.

Epiphany *(January 6):* We celebrate the visit of the three wise men to the infant Jesus.

Baptism of the Lord *(Sunday after Epiphany):* This marks the beginning of Jesus' public life.

Presentation *(February 2):* When the infant Jesus was brought to the Temple of Jerusalem.

Chair of Peter *(February 22):* This ancient feast reminds us of the unity our Church finds in the Pope.

Saint Joseph *(March 19):* We remember Joseph, the foster father of Jesus and guardian of the universal Church.

The Annunciation *(March 25):* When Gabriel came to Mary to tell her she would be the Mother of Jesus. Mary agreed to God's plan, and on this day Jesus began his life on earth, as a tiny unborn child inside his Mother.

Holy Week *(date varies):* We commemorate the Passion and death of Jesus.

Easter *(date varies):* We celebrate the Resurrection of Jesus.

Ascension *(forty days after Easter):* We commemorate the day Jesus returned to his Father in Heaven.

Visitation *(May 31):* Mary visited Elizabeth, who was pregnant with Saint John the Baptist. Saint Elizabeth was filled with the Holy Spirit and knew that Mary was the Mother of the Savior.

Pentecost *(fifty days after Easter):* We celebrate the birthday of the Church when the Holy Spirit descended on the apostles.

Holy Trinity *(Sunday after Pentecost):* We celebrate the mystery of the three Persons in One God.

Corpus Christi *(Thursday after Holy Trinity Sunday):* These words are Latin for ''the Body of Christ''. This feast honors Jesus in the Blessed Sacrament.

Sacred Heart *(Friday after second Sunday after Pentecost):* Jesus revealed to Saint Margaret Mary his Sacred Heart, wounded by sin, yet burning with love for men. He asked that men remember that he is a God of love, longing to forgive sinners. This feast

day reminds us of the loving Heart of Jesus.

Birth of John the Baptist *(June 24):* Usually a saint's feast is celebrated around the date of his death. For Saint John the Baptist we also celebrate his birth because of his special role as the herald of Jesus.

The Transfiguration *(August 6):* We commemorate the day Jesus appeared in glory on Mount Tabor.

The Assumption *(August 15):* The day Mary was taken body and soul into Heaven.

The Queenship of Mary *(August 22):* We honor Our Lady as Queen of Heaven and earth.

Beheading of Saint John the Baptist *(August 29):* We commemorate the death of John the Baptist.

Birth of Mary *(September 8):* Our Lady's birthday is celebrated because of her importance as the Mother of Jesus.

The Triumph of the Cross *(September 14):* On this day we recall that the holy Cross is the sign of our salvation.

Saints Michael, Raphael, Gabriel *(September 29):* These three archangels all are mentioned in the Sacred Scripture as powerful servants of God.

Guardian Angels *(October 2):* We honor the heavenly protector God has given to each one of us.

All Saints *(November 1):* On this day we praise God for all the saints, both those who are known to the Church, and those who are unknown.

All Souls *(November 2):* We pray for the souls in Purgatory, especially those of our family and friends who have died.

Christ the King *(last Sunday of the Church year):* We honor Jesus as King of Heaven and earth. We ask him to rule in our hearts, our homes, and our country.

Immaculate Conception *(December 8):* We

rejoice that, from the moment she began life within the womb of her mother, Mary's soul was kept free from original sin.

Christmas *(December 25):* The birth of Jesus.

Holy Family *(first Sunday after Christmas):* On this day we recall the perfect family life of Jesus, Mary, and Joseph. We ask them to help our family members to love one another and grow in holiness.

WORDS TO KNOW

ANGEL: a pure spirit with intellect and will.

ANNUNCIATION: God's announcement to Mary through the Archangel Gabriel that she was chosen to be the Mother of the Son of God.

APOSTLES' CREED: a prayer which contains the chief truths of the Catholic faith.

APOSTOLIC: connected with the apostles.

ASCENSION: Christ's visible departure from earth and going up into Heaven.

ASSUMPTION: the taking up into Heaven of the body and soul of Mary.

BISHOP: a successor to the apostles; leader in the Church.

BLASPHEMY: speaking about or to God in a scornful or irreverent way.

CARDINAL: a person, usually a bishop, selected by the Pope to belong to a special group in the leadership of the Church.

CATHOLIC: universal.

COMFORTER: a name given to the Holy Spirit.

CREATE: to make from nothing.

DEMON: a fallen or bad angel.

DIOCESE: a territory over which a bishop rules.

DIVINITY: having the divine nature.

ETERNAL LIFE: life lasting for ever.

EVANGELIZATION: spreading of the gospel message.

FAITH: a God-given power and habit by which we believe in him and all he has revealed. Also the body of truths we believe.

FORGIVENESS: pardon for a wrong done.

FREE WILL: the ability to make a choice.

GENERAL JUDGMENT: the event at the end of the world when everyone's eternal destiny will be made known to all.

GRACE: any gift from God; sanctifying grace is God's life in our souls.

HOLY: belonging to God.

IMMACULATE CONCEPTION: the special privilege that God gave to Mary by which she was free from original sin from the first moment of her life.

INCARNATION: the taking on of a human nature in time by the Son of God.

INFALLIBILITY: freedom from error in teaching the universal Church in matters of faith and morals.

MAGNIFICAT: Mary's song of praise to God.

MARKS OF THE CHURCH: the four characteristics of the Church by which it is recognized as the true Church of Christ.

MYSTERY: a divinely revealed truth which we can never fully understand.

MYSTICAL BODY: the Church; the union of the members of the Church with each other and Christ.

NATIVITY: day of birth, as the birth of Jesus Christ.

NATURE: the essence of a thing; what it is.

ONE: united in all important matters.

ORIGINAL SIN: the sin of Adam because of which we are born without grace.

PARABLE: a story used to teach.

PARTICULAR JUDGMENT: the judgment of a person by Christ immediately after death.

PASSOVER: the Jewish feast commemorating the deliverance of the Israelites from Egypt.

PENTECOST: the descent of the Holy Spirit upon the apostles.

PERSON: a being with intellect and will.

PROPHET: a messenger sent by God.

PURE SPIRIT: a being without a body.

RESURRECTION OF THE BODY: the rising of the body to be reunited with the soul at the end of the world.

REVELATION: the truths of faith which God has made known to us through Scripture and Tradition.

ROSARY: a special prayer to Mary, often using special beads and consisting of praying the Apostles' Creed, the Our Father, the Hail Mary, the Glory be, and the Hail Holy Queen, while thinking about scenes from the lives of Jesus and Mary.

SACRAMENT: a sign instituted by Jesus that gives us grace.

SACRIFICE: the offering up of something to God.

SANCTIFIER: a name given to the Holy Spirit.

SANCTIFY: to make holy.

SOUL: the spirit of a man.

TEN COMMANDMENTS: the laws given to us by God.

TRADITION: the handing on through the centuries of the whole of divine revelation, including the truths contained in Sacred Scripture.

TRANSFIGURATION: the glorious change in Jesus' appearance when he revealed something of his divinity to Peter, James, and John.

TRINITY: three Divine Persons in one God.

PRAYERS

THE SIGN OF THE CROSS

In the name of the Father, and of the Son, and of the Holy Spirit. *Amen*.

OUR FATHER

Our Father who art in Heaven, hallowed be thy Name. Thy Kingdom come, thy will be done on earth as it is in Heaven. Give us this day our daily bread, and forgive us our trespasses, as we forgive those who trespass against us, and lead us not into temptation, but deliver us from evil. *Amen*.

HAIL MARY

Hail Mary, full of grace, the Lord is with thee. Blessed art thou among women, and blessed is the fruit of thy womb, Jesus.

Holy Mary, Mother of God, pray for us sinners now and at the hour of our death. *Amen*.

GLORY BE

Glory be to the Father, and to the Son, and to the Holy Spirit. As it was in the beginning, is now, and ever shall be, world without end. *Amen*.

MORNING OFFERING

O Jesus, through the Immaculate Heart of Mary I offer thee my prayers, works, joys, and sufferings of this day in union with the Holy Sacrifice of the Mass throughout the world. I offer them for all the intentions of thy Sacred Heart: the salvation of souls, reparation for sin, the reunion of all Christians. I offer them for the intentions of our Bishops and of all Apostles of Prayer, and in particular for those recommended by our Holy Father this month.

THE APOSTLES' CREED

I believe in God, the Father almighty, Creator of Heaven and earth; and in Jesus Christ, his only Son, Our Lord, who was conceived by the Holy Spirit, born of the Virgin Mary, suffered under Pontius Pilate, was crucified, died, and was buried. He descended into Hell; the third day he rose again from the dead. He ascended into Heaven, and is seated at the right hand of God, the Father almighty. From thence he shall come to judge the living and the dead.

I believe in the Holy Spirit, the Holy Catholic Church, the Communion of Saints, the forgiveness of sins, the resurrection of the body, and life everlasting. *Amen*.

ACT OF CONTRITION

O my God, I am heartily sorry for having offended thee. I detest all my sins because of thy just punishments, but most of all because they offend thee, my God, who art all good and deserving of all my love. I firmly resolve, with the help of thy grace, to confess my sins, to do penance, and to amend my life. *Amen*.

ACT OF FAITH

O my God, I firmly believe that thou art one God in three Divine Persons, Father, Son, and Holy Spirit; I believe that thy Divine Son became man and died for our sins, and that he will come to judge the living and the dead. I believe these and all the truths that the Holy Catholic Church teaches, because thou hast revealed them, who can neither deceive nor be deceived.

ACT OF HOPE

O my God, relying on thy infinite goodness and promises, I hope to obtain pardon of my sins, the help of thy grace, and life everlasting, through the merits of Jesus Christ, my Lord and Redeemer.

ACT OF LOVE

O my God, I love thee above all things, with my whole heart and soul, because thou art all good and worthy of all love. I love my neighbor as myself for the love of thee. I forgive all who have injured me and ask pardon of all whom I have injured.

MYSTERIES OF THE ROSARY

The Joyful Mysteries

1. The Annunciation.
2. The Visitation.
3. The Nativity.
4. The Presentation.
5. The Finding in the Temple.

The Sorrowful Mysteries

1. The Agony in the Garden.
2. The Scourging at the Pillar.
3. The Crowning with Thorns.
4. The Carrying of the Cross.
5. The Crucifixion.

The Glorious Mysteries

1. The Resurrection.
2. The Ascension.
3. The Descent of the Holy Spirit.
4. The Assumption.
5. The Coronation.

THE STATIONS OF THE CROSS

1. Jesus is condemned to death.
2. Jesus carries his Cross.
3. Jesus falls the first time.
4. Jesus meets his Mother.
5. Jesus is helped by Simon of Cyrene.
6. Veronica wipes the face of Jesus.
7. Jesus falls a second time.
8. Jesus speaks to the women.
9. Jesus falls a third time.
10. Jesus is stripped of his clothes.
11. Jesus is nailed to the Cross.
12. Jesus dies on the Cross.
13. Jesus is taken down from the Cross.
14. Jesus is placed in the tomb.

THE ANGELUS

V. *The angel of the Lord declared unto Mary.*
R. And she conceived of the Holy Spirit.
   Hail Mary. . . .

V. *Behold the handmaid of the Lord.*
R. Be it done to me according to thy word.
   Hail Mary. . . .

V. *And the Word was made flesh.*
R. And dwelt among us.
   Hail Mary. . . .

V. *Pray for us, O holy Mother of God.*
R. That we may be made worthy of the promises of Christ.

Let us pray. Pour forth, we beseech thee, O Lord, thy grace into our hearts, that we, to whom the Incarnation of Christ thy Son was made known by the message of an angel, may by his Passion and Cross be brought to the glory of his Resurrection. Through the same Christ Our Lord. *Amen.*

MEMORARE

Remember, O most gracious Virgin Mary, that never was it known that anyone who fled to thy protection, implored thy help, or sought thy intercession, was left unaided. Inspired with this confidence, I fly unto thee, O Virgin of Virgins, my Mother: to thee do I come, before thee I stand, sinful and sorrowful. O Mother of the Word Incarnate, despise not my petitions, but in thy mercy hear and answer me. *Amen.*

PRAYER TO ST. MICHAEL

St. Michael, the Archangel, defend us in battle. Be our protection against the wickedness and snares of the devil. May God rebuke him, we humbly pray, and do thou, O prince of the Heavenly hosts, by the power of God, thrust into Hell Satan and the other evil spirits who prowl about the world seeking the ruin of souls. *Amen.*

ART CREDITS

BERLIN-DAHLEM STAATLICHE MUSEUM:

100   *The Merciful One*, 11th—12th century Byzantine mosaic

PHOTOGRAPHS:

93   Victor Puccetti
96   UPI/Bettman

OTHERS:

73   *Shroud of Turin*, Holy Shroud Guild, Bronx, N.Y. 10451
74   *Shroud of Turin*, Holy Shroud Guild, Bronx, N.Y. 10451
111 *Our Lady of Guadalupe*